150 Best Dips & Salsas

Plus Recipes for Chips, Flatbreads and More

Judith Finlayson & Jordan Wagman

D0565227

Robert
ROSE

For complete cataloguing information, see page 192.

Disclaimer
The recipes in this book have been carefully tested by our kitchen and our tasters. To the best of our knowledge, they are safe and nutritious for ordinary use and users. For those people with food or other allergies, or who have special food requirements or health issues, please read the suggested contents of each recipe carefully and determine whether or not they may create a problem for you. All recipes are used at the risk of the consumer.

We cannot be responsible for any hazards, loss or damage that may occur as a result of any recipe use.

For those with special needs, allergies, requirements or health problems, in the event of any doubt, please contact your medical adviser prior to the use of any recipe.

Design and Production: Kevin Cockburn/PageWave Graphics Inc.
Editor: Carol Sherman
Copy Editor: Karen Campbell-Sheviak
Recipe Tester: Jennifer MacKenzie

Cover Photography: Colin Erricson
Associate Photographer: Matt Johannsson
Food Styling: Kathryn Robertson
Prop Styling: Charlene Erricson

Interior Photography:
Photos by Colin Erricson; except *Sumptuous Spinach and Artichoke Dip, Feta and Roasted Red Pepper Dip* and *Tonnato, Tuna Tapenade, Nippy Oyster and Bacon Dip* with *Crisp Potato Wedges,* and *Black Bean and Salsa Dip* by Mark T. Shapiro; *Tzatziki* © iStockphoto.com/IngridHS; *Fresh Tomato Salsa* © iStockphoto.com/tacojim; *Guacamole* © iStockphoto.com/cobraphoto; *Easy Hummus* © iStockphoto.com/tashka2000

The publisher gratefully acknowledges the financial support of our publishing program by the Government of Canada through the Canada Book Fund.

Published by Robert Rose Inc.
120 Eglinton Avenue East, Suite 800, Toronto, Ontario, Canada M4P 1E2
Tel: (416) 322-6552 Fax: (416) 322-6936
www.robertrose.ca

Printed and bound in USA

1 2 3 4 5 6 7 8 9 CW 22 21 20 19 18 17 16 15 14

Contents

Introduction

If there are two words that define entertaining today, it's dips and salsas. Not only do these tasty tidbits fit the bill for easy entertaining — gathering round the kitchen island, sampling a potpourri of textures and flavors — but they are also the most sociable of recipes. There is nothing like flavorsome nibblies and a refreshing libation to stimulate conversation and encourage conviviality. This combination is a great catalyst for getting any gathering off to a good start.

Dips (and their kissing cousins, slightly thicker spreads) play key roles in many cultures. Some have traveled internationally. Middle Eastern hummus and baba ghanouj, Greek tzatziki, and French tapenade, to name just a few — are now regularly enjoyed in many different parts of the world. Most dips are easy to make and can be prepared ahead of time. They are happily coupled with store-bought dippers, such as pita bread or sliced baguette, but if you feel like bumping things up a notch, they are very amenable to more elaborate pairings such as Yogurt Flatbread (page 174) or Salt-Roasted Potatoes (page 162). Like dips, salsas work well with simple accompaniments, such as tortilla chips, while also lending themselves to a fancier finish.

Although the word *salsa* translates as "sauce," most people know salsa as guacamole or pico de gallo, a tomato-based dip. Both are treated as dips and commonly enjoyed with tortilla chips. (In Mexico, where guacamole is traditionally made in a *molcajete*, it is chunkier than most northern versions.) But salsas, which are traditionally associated with Mexico and Latin America, are a great deal more. With a rainbow of colors and a wide array of textures and flavors from salty and sweet to spicy and sour, salsas are the ultimate condiment. Made with fresh, seasonal ingredients, they are refreshing and nutritious. As you'll see, they can contain many different kinds of ingredients, from raw bananas and tropical fruits to cooked beans and corn, and dried fruit. There are an infinite number of blends.

In this book, you'll find many recipes for salsas that are very simple to make but mouthwateringly delicious. Have some fun and create a first-course salsa bar. Prepare two or three salsa recipes; most will certainly be happily coupled with traditional tortilla chips but if you're so inclined, you can have fun thinking out-of-the-box in terms of what to serve as accompaniments. Depending on their flavor profile, salsas can be paired with a variety of dippers. Cheese or Corn Arepas (pages 179 and 180), Green Plantain Chips (page 167) and Fresh Corn Cakes (page 166) are all good choices. Rice crackers or cucumber slices also come to mind. The range of compatible combinations is practically endless.

In keeping with the spirit of easy entertaining, we've also included a chapter of dessert dips and salsas. These sweet treats are the perfect solution for those times when you want to entertain friends without preparing an entire meal. If you have ever thought of having a "champagne and dessert" get together, now is the time.

In selecting these recipes, we made sure we were satisfying as many dietary preferences as possible, from the strictest vegans to wide-ranging omnivores. Most of the recipes are inherently gluten-free. However, in those cases where a recipe contained gluten (or an ingredient that might contain gluten) we have provided a gluten-free alternative. And because we feel so passionately about their ability to create an exceptional gustatory experience, we even included an entire chapter of recipes for making perfect complements to the dips and salsas in this book. Although store-bought versions are widely available, there is no substitute for the goodness of homemade. Make your own crostini, bagel chips, potato chips or flatbread (including a gluten-free version) and you'll create a fabulous finish for the dips, spreads and salsas in this book.

Enjoy!

— *Judith Finlayson and Jordan Wagman*

Vegetable Dips and Spreads

Canary Island Red Pepper Mojo

This is a toned-down variation on a classic hot sauce that is served in the Canary Islands. There it often accompanies a traditional dish known as wrinkled potatoes. For a spectacular appetizer, cook up a batch of Salt-Roasted Potatoes (page 162), put them on skewers and use this Mojo as a dipping sauce. Boiled or grilled shrimp make equally delicious dippers.

Makes about ⅔ cup (150 mL)

Tips

Use the kind of red chile you have easy access to. Long red or Thai bird's eye both work well in this recipe. If you're heat adverse, seed and devein the chile before using.

Hot paprika is made from a variety of *Capsicum annuum* that is hot. If Spanish in origin it will be identified as *pecante*; if Hungarian it will be categorized as *Eros*. If you don't have hot paprika, use ¾ tsp (3 mL) sweet paprika and ¼ tsp (1 mL) cayenne pepper for the quantity called for here.

- **Food processor**

1	long red chile, chopped (see Tips, left)	1
1 tsp	hot paprika (see Tips, left)	5 mL
1 tsp	ground cumin (see Tip, page 12)	5 mL
2	cloves garlic, chopped	2
2	roasted red bell peppers, quartered (see Tip, page 30) or store-bought	2
3 tbsp	red wine vinegar	45 mL
½ cup	extra virgin olive oil	125 mL
	Salt	

1. In food processor fitted with metal blade, pulse chile pepper, paprika, cumin, garlic, roasted peppers and vinegar until chopped and blended, about 5 times. With motor running, add olive oil through feed tube and process until smoothly blended, about 1 minute. Season to taste with salt. Transfer to a bowl and serve.

Avocado Ancho Chile Dip

This dip is a variation on the theme of guacamole and is wonderful with tortilla chips. It also makes a great finish for tacos.

Makes about 1 cup (250 mL)

Tip

Pommery mustard is a French mustard also known as Moutarde de Meaux. It is similar in flavor to Dijon mustard, but we have specified it here because it adds a pleasant grainy texture to this dip.

• **Food processor**

1	avocado, cut into chunks (about 1 cup/250 mL)	1
¼ cup	mayonnaise	60 mL
1 tbsp	cream cheese	15 mL
1 tsp	rice wine vinegar	5 mL
1 tsp	grainy (Pommery) mustard (see Tip, left)	5 mL
¼ tsp	salt	1 mL
¼ tsp	ancho chile powder	1 mL
¼ tsp	liquid honey	1 mL

1. In food processor fitted with metal blade, pulse avocado, mayonnaise, cream cheese, vinegar, mustard, salt, ancho chile and honey until smooth. Transfer to a serving bowl. Serve immediately or cover with plastic wrap, pressing down on surface of dip, and refrigerate for up to 4 hours.

Easy Tahini Dip

This recipe can be put together in a jiffy with ingredients you're likely to have on hand, yet is exotic and delicious enough to seem like you went to a great deal of trouble. Serve with warm pita bread or any Middle Eastern flatbread.

Makes about 1¾ cups (425 mL)

Tip

For best flavor, toast and grind cumin yourself. *To toast seeds:* Place seeds in a dry skillet over medium heat and cook, stirring, until fragrant, about 3 minutes. Immediately transfer to a mortar or a spice grinder and grind.

- **Food processor**

1 cup	packed Italian flat-leaf parsley leaves	250 mL
½ cup	tahini	125 mL
½ cup	freshly squeezed lemon juice	125 mL
¼ cup	cold water	60 mL
2	cloves garlic, coarsely chopped	2
1 tsp	salt	5 mL
¼ tsp	ground cumin (see Tip, left)	1 mL
	Freshly ground black pepper	

1. In food processor fitted with metal blade, process parsley, tahini, lemon juice, water, garlic, salt and cumin until smoothly blended, about 30 seconds. Season to taste with pepper. Transfer to a serving bowl. Serve at room temperature.

Eggplant Caviar

This spread/dip is very easy to make and delicious. Not only is it a great entertaining dish, it's also wonderful to have on hand for snacking since it is loaded with nutrients. Serve with sliced baguette, warm pita bread or sliced veggies.

Makes about 2½ cups (625 mL)

Tips

We always use Italian flat-leaf parsley because it has so much more flavor than the curly leaf variety. Unless the stems or sprigs are specifically called for, use only the tender leaves.

Make sure you have thoroughly dried the herbs (patting between layers of paper towels or in a salad spinner) before adding to the food processor; otherwise your spread may be watery.

- **Preheat oven to 400°F (200°C)**
- **Food processor**

1	medium eggplant (about 1 lb/500 g)	1
1 cup	cherry tomatoes	250 mL
½ cup	Italian flat-leaf parsley leaves (see Tips, left)	125 mL
4	cloves garlic	4
4	green onions, white part only, cut into chunks	4
3 tbsp	freshly squeezed lemon juice	45 mL
2 tbsp	extra virgin olive oil	30 mL
	Salt and freshly ground black pepper	

1. Prick eggplant in several places with a fork. Place on a baking sheet and bake in preheated oven until blackened and softened, about 45 minutes. Set aside.

2. Scoop out eggplant flesh and place in food processor fitted with metal blade. Discard skin and stem. Add tomatoes, parsley, garlic, green onions, lemon juice, olive oil and salt and pepper to taste. Process until smooth.

3. Transfer to a bowl. Cover and refrigerate for at least 3 hours until thoroughly chilled or for up to 2 days.

Baba Ghanouj

No mezes platter would be complete without a bowl of this ambrosial eggplant dip. We find some versions a bit overpowering so we have tamed the stronger flavors in this version. Serve with pita triangles or crudités. If you have any leftover, it makes a great spread for sandwiches and a fabulous topping for burgers or meat patties.

Makes about 2 cups (500 mL)

Tips

Make an effort to get Greek-style yogurt, also known as "pressed." It is lusciously thick and adds beautiful depth to this and many other dishes. If you can't find Greek yogurt, you can make your own. *To make Greek-Style yogurt:* Line a sieve with a double layer of cheesecloth or paper towels. Add plain yogurt, cover and refrigerate overnight. The watery component will have drained out and you will be be left with lovely thick yogurt.

It is usually more convenient to cook eggplant for baba ghanouj in the oven. However, if it is the season, you may want to try grilling it on the barbecue. The smoky taste adds great flavor to the dip and is the traditional cooking method in the Middle East, where this dip originates.

- **Preheat oven to 400°F (200°C)**
- **Food processor**

1	large eggplant (about 1½ lbs/750 g)	1
½ cup	plain yogurt, preferably Greek-style (pressed) (see Tips, left)	125 mL
¼ cup	tahini	60 mL
¼ cup	freshly squeezed lemon juice	60 mL
¼ cup	Italian flat-leaf parsley leaves	60 mL
2	cloves garlic, coarsely chopped	2
½ tsp	salt	2 mL
	Finely chopped parsley, optional	

1. Prick eggplant in several places with a fork. Place on a baking sheet and bake in preheated oven until blackened and soft, about 1 hour. Alternatively, place on a gas or charcoal grill preheated to high and cook, turning several times, until skin is blackened and blistered and eggplant is very soft, about 40 minutes (see Tips, left). Let cool.

2. Scoop out eggplant flesh and place in food processor fitted with metal blade. Discard skin and stem. Add yogurt, tahini, lemon juice, parsley, garlic and salt and process until smooth, about 1 minute.

3. Transfer to a serving dish and garnish with additional parsley, if using. Serve at room temperature or cover and refrigerate for up to 2 days.

Greek-Style Garlic-Spiked Potato Dip

This version of the Greek sauce skordalia is made with mashed potatoes rather than bread. It is particularly delicious. Serve with warm pita, Crisp Pita Bread (page 172) or crudités.

Makes about 2 cups (500 mL)

Tips

For the best flavor, buy almonds with the skin on and blanch them yourself. *To blanch almonds:* Drop almonds in a pot of rapidly boiling water and boil until the skins start to pucker. Transfer to a colander and rinse well under cold running water. Using your hands, pop the almonds out of their skins. Place on paper towels and let dry for at least 10 minutes.

To toast almonds: In a skillet over medium-high heat add enough almonds just to cover the bottom of the skillet and, stirring constantly, toast until fragrant and golden brown, 2 to 3 minutes.

Refrigerating this dip will cause it to congeal and dramatically intensify the flavor of the garlic. It is best served soon after it is made, at room temperature.

- **Food processor**

1 lb	russet (Idaho) potatoes, boiled in their skins, cooled, peeled and coarsely chopped (about 2)	500 g
4	cloves garlic, coarsely chopped	4
¼ cup	freshly squeezed lemon juice	60 mL
½ cup	coarsely chopped blanched almonds, toasted (see Tips, left)	125 mL
½ cup	extra virgin olive oil	125 mL
	Salt and freshly ground black pepper	
	Finely chopped parsley	

1. In food processor fitted with metal blade, process garlic until finely chopped, stopping and scraping down sides of the bowl. Add potatoes and pulse to blend, about 10 times. Add lemon juice and almonds and pulse to blend, about 5 times. With motor running, add olive oil through the feed tube and process until mixture is smooth and blended. Season to taste with salt and pepper.

2. Transfer to serving bowl. Garnish with parsley and serve immediately at room temperature.

Roasted Pepper and Sweet Potato Dip

Roasting vegetables intensifies their flavors and brings out inherent sweetness. This dip is basically a medley of healthful vegetables, roasted and blended, with minimal accents. It's chock full of nutrition and delicious to boot. Serve with tortilla chips, warm pita, rice crackers or even sliced baguette.

Makes about 3 cups (750 mL)

Tips

It will take about 20 minutes for the jalapeño to blister, 30 minutes for the bell pepper and tomato and about 50 minutes for the sweet potato to become soft.

For best flavor, toast and grind cumin yourself. *To toast seeds:* Place seeds in a dry skillet over medium heat and cook, stirring, until fragrant, about 3 minutes. Immediately transfer to a mortar or a spice grinder and grind.

We always use flat-leaf rather than curly parsley because it has more flavor.

- **Preheat oven to 400°F (200°C)**
- **Food processor**

1	sweet potato (about 8 oz/250 g)	1
1	green bell pepper	1
1	large tomato, halved, cut side brushed with olive oil	1
3	cloves garlic, unpeeled	3
1	jalapeño pepper, optional	1
2 tsp	extra virgin olive oil	10 mL
1 tsp	ground cumin (see Tips, left)	5 mL
	Salt and freshly ground black pepper	
2 tbsp	finely chopped Italian flat-leaf parsley leaves	30 mL

1. On a rimmed baking sheet, in preheated oven, roast sweet potato, bell pepper, tomato, garlic, and jalapeño, if using. Turn bell pepper and jalapeño several times to blacken on all sides and when they are nicely blistered, transfer to a bowl, cover with a plate and let sweat. Turn garlic once and when very soft, remove from oven and let cool. When tomato is softened and skin looks very wizened remove from oven and let cool. When sweet potato is soft, remove from oven and let cool (see Tips, left).

2. When cool enough to handle, peel pepper(s) and cut into chunks. Squeeze garlic out of skins. Remove skin from tomatoes and cut out core. Scoop sweet potato out of skin. Discard skins and core.

3. Transfer pepper(s), garlic, tomato and sweet potato to a food processor fitted with metal blade. Add olive oil, cumin, and salt and pepper to taste. Process until smooth and blended, about 1 minute. Transfer to a serving bowl and garnish with parsley. Serve warm.

Green Olive Tapenade

If you're looking for something a little different, try this. It is much lighter than the traditional tapenade made with black olives. Served on crackers, Basic Crostini (page 176) or sliced baguette, it makes a wonderful accompaniment to cocktails in the garden on a warm summer night.

Makes about 1 cup (250 mL)

Tip

For best results use nonpareil capers. They are the smallest version of the edible flower buds and they have the best flavor and most pleasing texture.

• **Food processor**

1 cup	pitted drained green olives	250 mL
¼ cup	fresh basil leaves	60 mL
2	cloves garlic, coarsely chopped	2
1 tbsp	drained capers (see Tip, left)	15 mL
¼ cup	extra virgin olive oil	60 mL
1 tbsp	freshly squeezed lemon juice	15 mL

1. In food processor fitted with metal blade, pulse olives, basil, garlic and capers until finely chopped. Add olive oil and lemon juice and pulse just until blended.

2. Transfer to a small serving bowl. Cover and refrigerate for at least 2 hours or for up to 3 days.

Grilled Scallion and Corn Dip

This dip is an amazing summertime recipe that is perfect on Basic Crostini (page 176), tortilla chips or crudités, such as bell peppers.

Makes about 1⅔ cups (400 mL)

Tips

Scallions, also known as green onions, are widely available and perfect raw where a subtle onion-note is needed. When grilled, they become smoky and contrast the sweetness of the corn beautifully.

To grill corn: Preheat barbecue grill to high. Grill ears of corn, husks on, rotating often until dark brown all over, about 20 minutes. Transfer to a plate and let cool for 5 minutes or until cool enough to handle. Remove husk and silks and, using a serrated knife, cut kernels from cob.

Chipotle peppers are smoked jalapeño peppers. They can be found dried (whole or ground) or combined with adobo sauce and canned.

- **Preheat barbecue to medium-high**
- **Food processor**

3	green onions (scallions) (see Tips, left)	3
½ tsp	olive oil	2 mL
1 cup	grilled corn kernels (see Tips, left)	250 mL
½ cup	rice vinegar	125 mL
¼ cup	water	60 mL
¼ cup	coarsely chopped fresh cilantro leaves	60 mL
2 tbsp	coarsely chopped cherry tomatoes	30 mL
2	cloves garlic	2
½ tsp	salt	2 mL
⅛ tsp	chipotle powder	0.5 mL
⅛ tsp	freshly ground black pepper	0.5 mL

1. In a bowl, combine green onions and oil to coat. Grill, turning often, until golden brown and soft, 4 to 5 minutes. Transfer to a food processor fitted with metal blade. Add corn, vinegar, water, cilantro, tomatoes, garlic, salt, chipotle and black pepper and pulse until smooth. Serve immediately or cover and refrigerate for up to 3 days.

Roasted Onion Dip

Serve beside pork dumplings or wontons for dipping. Or it's great with just Homemade Potato Chips (page 165).

Makes about 1½ cups (375 mL)

Tips

Shallots are wonderful when roasted, too. Use 3 to 4 shallots per onion. Adjust the cooking time slightly and cook for about 45 minutes.

If you have problems consuming gluten, check to make sure your ketchup is a gluten-free brand.

● **Preheat oven to 400°F (200°C)**

2	medium onions (see Tips, left)	2
½ tsp	minced capers	2 mL
1 tbsp	balsamic vinegar	15 mL
1 tbsp	tomato ketchup (see Tips, left)	15 mL
¼ tsp	fresh rosemary leaves	1 mL
¼ tsp	freshly ground black pepper	1 mL

1. Place onions on a baking sheet and roast in preheated oven until soft, about 1 hour. Let cool to room temperature, then peel and mince. (You should have 1 cup/250 mL.)

2. In a bowl, combine onions, capers, vinegar, ketchup, rosemary and pepper. Serve immediately or refrigerate for up to 3 days.

Mojo de Cilantro

If you've been traveling in the Canary Islands and have enjoyed a cilantro sauce that seems to be ubiquitous there, here's a version you can make at home. It makes a delicious dip for Salt-Roasted Potatoes (page 162), boiled or grilled shrimp or even Homemade Potato Chips (page 165).

Makes about ½ cup (125 mL)

Tips

If you have a mini-bowl attachment for your food processor, this is an ideal recipe for it.

For best flavor, toast and grind cumin yourself. *To toast seeds:* Place seeds in a dry skillet over medium heat and cook, stirring, until fragrant, about 3 minutes. Immediately transfer to a mortar or a spice grinder and grind.

• **Food processor (see Tips, left)**

2 cups	packed fresh cilantro leaves	500 mL
1 tbsp	white wine vinegar	15 mL
2	cloves garlic, quartered	2
1	long red or green chile pepper, quartered	1
1 tsp	ground cumin (see Tips, left)	5 mL
⅓ cup	extra virgin olive oil	75 mL
	Salt and freshly ground black pepper	

1. In food processor fitted with metal blade or mini bowl attachment, pulse cilantro, vinegar, garlic, chile pepper and cumin until finely chopped, stopping and scraping down sides of bowl as necessary. With motor running, slowly add oil through feed tube and process just until blended. Season to taste with salt and pepper.

2. Transfer to a small serving bowl and set aside for 30 minutes to allow flavors to meld. Serve at room temperature.

Roasted Tomato and Pumpkin Seed Dip

If you're looking for something a little different, try this Mexican-inspired dip. It is as nutritious as it is tasty. Serve with tostadas or tortilla chips.

Makes about 2¼ cups (550 mL)

Tips

One jalapeño produces a timidly spiced dip. If you like heat, add more to suit your taste.

Roasted tomatoes freeze very well so it's a good idea to make extra to have on hand. Roast tomatoes and let cool to room temperature. Transfer to a freezer bag and store frozen until needed for up to 3 months.

- **Preheat oven to 400°F (200°C)**
- **Food processor**

10	plum tomatoes, halved lengthwise	10
1 tbsp	olive oil	15 mL
1 tsp	dried oregano	5 mL
½ cup	hulled pumpkin seeds (pepitas)	125 mL
2 cups	cooked drained white beans	500 mL
4	green onions, white part with a bit of green, cut into chunks	4
¼ cup	coarsely chopped cilantro	60 mL
1 to 3	jalapeño peppers, seeded and quartered (see Tips, left)	1 to 3
1 tsp	salt	5 mL
	Freshly ground black pepper	

1. In a bowl, combine halved tomatoes and olive oil. Toss until evenly coated. Place on a baking sheet cut side up and sprinkle evenly with oregano. Roast in preheated oven until soft and just starting to brown around the edges, about 20 minutes. Set aside.

2. Meanwhile, in a skillet over medium heat, toast pumpkin seeds until fragrant and they begin to pop, about 3 minutes. Transfer to a food processor fitted with metal blade.

3. Add beans, green onions, cilantro, jalapeño pepper to taste, salt and reserved tomatoes. Process until smooth. Season to taste with pepper.

4. Transfer to a serving bowl. Serve immediately or cover and refrigerate for up to 2 days. If refrigerated, let stand at room temperature for about 20 minutes before serving to allow the flavors to develop.

Roasted Tomato Dip

Roasted tomatoes take on a sweet smoky flavor, try them once and you'll be hooked. Best served with crudités or Crisp Pita Bread (page 172) for dipping.

Makes about 1½ cups (375 mL)

Tip

Roasted tomatoes freeze very well so it's a good idea to make extra to have on hand. Roast tomatoes and let cool to room temperature. Transfer to a freezer bag and store frozen until needed, for up to 3 months.

- **Preheat oven to 450°F (230°C)**
- **Food processor**

2 cups	cubed ripe tomatoes	500 mL
1 tsp	extra virgin olive oil	5 mL
½ tsp	salt	2 mL
2 tbsp	finely diced onion	30 mL
2 tbsp	chopped fresh basil leaves	30 mL
1 tsp	balsamic vinegar	5 mL
½ tsp	freshly ground black pepper	2 mL

1. On a rimmed baking sheet, combine tomatoes, oil and salt. Roast in preheated oven until soft, about 10 minutes. Turn oven to broil and roast tomatoes until golden brown, about 5 minutes (see Tip, left).

2. Transfer tomato mixture to food processor fitted with metal blade. Add onion, basil, vinegar and pepper and pulse until smooth. Serve immediately or cover and refrigerate for up to 3 days.

Mushroom Tomato Spread

When served with raw button mushrooms or spread on warm Basic Crostini (page 176), this easy spread is very comforting.

Makes about 1½ cups (375 mL)

Tip

Mushrooms contain a high proportion of water. By adding salt early in the cooking process water will be leached out of the mushrooms and evaporate, leaving them dry and flavorful.

• Food processor

1 tbsp	olive oil	15 mL
1 tbsp	unsalted butter	15 mL
4 cups	sliced button mushrooms	1 L
2 tbsp	coarsely chopped drained oil-packed sun-dried tomatoes	30 mL
2	thyme sprigs	2
1 tsp	salt	5 mL
¼ cup	soft goat cheese	60 mL
1 tbsp	sherry vinegar	15 mL
1 tsp	thinly sliced green onions	5 mL

1. In a saucepan, heat oil and butter over medium heat. Add mushrooms, tomatoes, thyme and salt and cook, stirring, until all liquid from mushrooms is evaporated, about 10 minutes (see Tip, left). Remove from heat and discard thyme sprigs. Add goat cheese, sherry and onions.

2. Transfer to a food processor fitted with metal blade and pulse until smooth. Transfer to a serving bowl.

Spinach Tofu Dip

Light and healthful, all this tasty dip needs is a crisp rice cracker to complete the experience.

Makes about 2 cups (500 mL)

Tip

Because this dip contains a significant quantity of spinach, which is likely to become soggy, we don't recommend storing it for longer than overnight.

● **Food processor**

8 oz	soft or medium tofu, cubed	250 g
6	green onions, white with a bit of green, cut into chunks	6
2	cloves garlic, quartered	2
1/4 cup	mayonnaise	60 mL
1/4 cup	sour cream	60 mL
1 tbsp	freshly squeezed lemon juice	15 mL
2 tsp	Dijon mustard	10 mL
1 tsp	salt	5 mL
8 cups	loosely packed baby spinach	2 L
	Freshly ground black pepper	

1. In food processor fitted with metal blade, process tofu, green onions, garlic, mayonnaise, sour cream, lemon juice, Dijon mustard and salt until smooth. Add spinach and pulse until very finely chopped and blended, about 10 times. Season to taste with pepper.

2. Transfer to a serving bowl. Cover and refrigerate for at least 1 hour to allow flavors to meld or overnight.

Springtime Dill Dip

Don't underestimate this dip because it is so easy to make. It is quite delicious accompanied by simple crudités such as cucumber slices, celery sticks, or blanched asparagus. It you want to bump things up a notch, serve it with Salt-Roasted Potatoes (page 162), an absolutely divine pairing.

Makes about 1 cup (250 mL)

Tips

If you have a mini-bowl attachment, it is ideal for this recipe.

When serving cold dips, particularly those that contain a high proportion of dairy, consider lining a deep platter with crushed ice and use it to surround the bowl. Arranging crudités over the ice will help to keep them nicely chilled as well.

• **Food processor (see Tips, left)**

½ cup	mayonnaise	125 mL
½ cup	plain Greek-style (pressed) yogurt (see Tips, page 14)	125 mL
½ cup	packed fresh dill fronds	125 mL
4	green onions, white part with a bit of green, cut into 2-inch (5 cm) pieces	4
½ tsp	salt	2 mL
	Freshly ground black pepper	

1. In food processor fitted with metal blade or mini bowl attachment, process mayonnaise, yogurt, dill, green onions, salt, and pepper to taste until smooth and blended, about 1 minute.

2. Transfer to a serving bowl and serve or cover and refrigerate overnight.

Creamy Watercress Dip

Make this garden-fresh dip when watercress is in season. Serve with crudités such as cucumber slices, carrot or celery sticks or hearts of romaine.

Makes about 1 cup (250 mL)

Tip

Because this dip contains watercress, which will become soggy, we don't recommend storing it for longer than overnight.

• **Food processor**

6 cups	packed watercress (leaves and tender stems, tough stems discarded)	1.5 L
6	green onions, white with a bit of green, cut into 2-inch (5 cm) lengths	6
4 oz	cream cheese, softened	125 g
2 tbsp	mayonnaise	30 mL
	Salt and freshly ground black pepper	

1. In food processor fitted with metal blade, pulse watercress and green onions until coarsely chopped. Add cream cheese and mayonnaise and process until smooth, about 30 seconds. Season to taste with salt and pepper and pulse to blend.

2. Transfer to a serving bowl. Cover and refrigerate for at least 1 hour to allow flavors to meld or overnight.

Roasted Fennel Dip

For those of you yet to experience the succulent flavor of roasted fennel, go out and buy one now. It's delicious! Serve this dip with wedges of raw fennel or with Roasted Potato Wedges (page 163) or Crisp Potato Wedges (see below). Parsnip Chips (page 171) and Taro Root Chips (page 170) would be wonderful too.

Makes about 1⅔ cups (400 mL)

Tips

We prefer to use full-fat sour cream in this recipe because it has a deeper flavor profile but if you prefer, use a lower-fat alternative.

White balsamic vinegar is, like the regular version, cooked to intensify its flavor. But it is aged only for a short period and maintains its light color, which makes it useful in recipes where a darker color and heavier flavor is not desirable. Look for it in well-stocked supermarkets.

- **Preheat oven to 450°F (230°C)**
- **Food processor**

Roasted Fennel Purée

1	fennel bulb, cut into quarters	1
2 tbsp	water	30 mL
1 tbsp	olive oil	15 mL
¼ tsp	salt	1 mL
½ cup	sour cream (see Tips, left)	125 mL
1 tbsp	white balsamic vinegar (see Tips, left)	15 mL
½ tsp	coarsely chopped fresh thyme leaves	2 mL
¼ tsp	grated lemon zest	1 mL

1. *Roasted Fennel Purée:* On a baking sheet, combine fennel bulb, water, olive oil and salt. Roast in preheated oven until fennel is caramelized and soft, about 40 minutes. Transfer to a food processor fitted with metal blade or use an immersion blender in a tall container and purée until smooth.

2. In a bowl, combine 1⅓ cups (325 mL) fennel purée, sour cream, vinegar, thyme and lemon zest. Serve immediately or cover and refrigerate for up to 3 days.

Crisp Potato Wedges

Bake the desired number of baking potatoes in a 400°F (200°C) oven for 1 hour. Set aside to cool. When you are ready to serve, preheat broiler. Cut each potato into 8 wedges and brush on all sides with olive oil. Place under preheated broiler until crisp and golden.

Peppery Peanut Dip

Here's a delicious and nutritious dip that is very easy to make. It is a perfect accompaniment to a platter of crudités. For something a little different, try serving fresh strawberries as dippers.

Makes about 1½ cups (375 mL)

Tip

If you have problems digesting gluten, substitute an equal quantity of gluten-free tamari for the soy sauce.

• **Food processor**

1 cup	peanut butter	250 mL
6	green onions, white part with a bit of green, cut into chunks	6
1	jalapeño pepper, seeded and quartered	1
8	fresh basil leaves (approx.)	8
2 tsp	finely grated lemon zest	10 mL
¼ cup	freshly squeezed lemon juice	60 mL
¼ cup	warm water (approx.)	60 mL
1 tbsp	soy sauce (see Tip, left)	15 mL

1. In food processor fitted with metal blade, process peanut butter, green onions, jalapeño pepper, basil, lemon zest and juice, water and soy sauce until smooth and blended. Add more warm water, if necessary, to make a smooth and creamy consistency. Transfer to a serving bowl and garnish with whole basil leaves.

Thai Peanut Dip

This versatile dip is wonderful with hot crisps, fresh spring rolls or crudités.

Makes about 2 cups (500 mL)

Tips

If you have trouble digesting gluten, look for gluten-free versions of soy sauce and hoisin sauce.

Be sure to use plain rice vinegar, not the seasoned variety, in this recipe.

• **Food processor**

1½ cups	roasted unsalted peanuts	375 mL
¾ cup	soy sauce (see Tips, left)	175 mL
¼ cup	hoisin sauce	60 mL
¼ cup	water	60 mL
1 tbsp	rice vinegar (see Tips, left)	15 mL
1 tsp	coarsely chopped fresh cilantro leaves	5 mL
1 tsp	coarsely chopped green onions	5 mL
½ tsp	hot pepper sauce	2 mL

1. In food processor fitted with metal blade, pulse nuts, soy sauce, hoisin, water, vinegar, cilantro, green onions and hot pepper sauce until smooth. Serve immediately or cover and refrigerate for up to 3 days.

Roasted Red Pepper Tzatziki

If you enjoy the fresh flavor of tzatziki but are looking for something a little different, try this. It makes a great dip for crudités and pita. For something more substantial, serve with a platter of boiled or grilled shrimp and provide wooden skewers for dipping. It also makes a great accompaniment to chicken kabobs.

Makes about 2 cups (500 mL)

Tips

To roast peppers: Preheat broiler. Place peppers on a baking sheet and broil, turning two or three times, until skin on all sides is blackened, about 25 minutes. Transfer to a heatproof bowl. Cover with a plate and let stand until cool. Remove and, using a sharp knife, lift skins off. Discard skins, core and seeds.

Be sure to use Greek-style yogurt (see Tips, page 32). Otherwise your dip will be too thin.

• **Food processor**

2	roasted red bell peppers, quartered (see Tips, left) or store-bought	2
1	field cucumber, seeded and cut into chunks, or 1/2 English cucumber, cut into chunks	1
6	green onions, white part with a bit of green, cut into chunks	6
1/2 cup	plain Greek-style (pressed) yogurt (see Tips, left)	125 mL
2	cloves garlic, coarsely chopped	2
1/2 tsp	ground cumin	2 mL
	Salt and freshly ground black pepper	

1. In food processor fitted with metal blade, process roasted peppers, cucumber, green onions, yogurt, garlic and cumin until smooth. Season to taste with salt and pepper.
2. Transfer to a serving bowl. Cover and refrigerate until thoroughly chilled or for up to 3 days.

Walnut Hummus

Vegan Friendly

If you're looking for something a little different, try this tasty spin on hummus, made with walnuts instead of chickpeas. It is particularly delicious served on a strip of crisp sweet red pepper, but also works well with other crudités, as well as pita bread.

Makes about 1½ cups (375 mL)

Tip

Because walnuts are particularly high in omega-3 fatty acids (which are very beneficial to your health) they become rancid relatively quickly. Always purchase walnuts from a trusted purveyor with rapid turnover and, just to be sure, taste before you buy.

• Food processor

1½ cups	walnut halves (see Tip, left)	375 mL
2 tbsp	tahini	30 mL
2 tbsp	freshly squeezed lemon juice	30 mL
1 tbsp	extra virgin olive oil	15 mL
1	clove garlic, chopped	1
½ tsp	hot paprika	2 mL
½ tsp	salt	2 mL
	Freshly ground black pepper	

1. In food processor fitted with metal blade, process walnuts, tahini, lemon juice, olive oil, garlic, paprika and salt until smooth, about 30 seconds, stopping and scraping down sides of the bowl as necessary. Season to taste with pepper and pulse to blend.

2. Transfer to a serving bowl. Serve immediately or cover and refrigerate for up to 1 day. If refrigerated, before serving, let stand at room temperature for about 20 minutes to allow the flavors to develop.

Tahini-Spiked Beet Spread

This Middle-Eastern-inspired spread is delightfully different and extremely nutritious. It's particularly delicious with grilled or toasted whole-grain pita bread, but plain baguette works well, too. It's great for entertaining because you can make it well ahead if you're rationing your time.

Makes about 1½ cups (375 mL)

Tips

To maintain the bright color of the beets, place 2 tbsp (30 mL) vinegar in a bowl. Roll scrubbed beets in the vinegar before roasting.

Be sure to use Greek-style yogurt, also known as "pressed." It is lusciously thick and adds beautiful depth to this and many other dishes. Greek yogurt is available in well-stocked supermarkets and specialty stores. If you can't find it, you can make your own. *To make Greek-style yogurt:* Line a sieve with a double layer of cheesecloth or paper towels. Add plain yogurt, cover and refrigerate overnight. The watery component will have drained out and you will be left with lovely thick yogurt.

Dip keeps, covered and refrigerated, for up to 3 days.

- **Preheat oven to 400°F (200°C)**

4	medium beets, scrubbed (see Tips, left)	4
	Olive oil	
⅓ cup	plain yogurt, preferably Greek-Style (see Tips, left)	75 mL
¼ cup	tahini	60 mL
¼ cup	fresh dill fronds	60 mL
2 tbsp	freshly squeezed lemon juice	30 mL
2	cloves garlic, coarsely chopped	2
1 tsp	salt	5 mL
	Freshly ground black pepper	

1. Place beets on a rimmed baking sheet or in a baking dish. Toss with oil and cover with foil. Roast in preheated oven until tender, about 1 hour. Remove from oven, spoon off 2 tbsp (30 mL) of the cooking juice and set aside. Let beets cool, then using a piece of paper towel, rub off skins. Coarsely chop.

2. In food processor fitted with metal blade, process beets, yogurt, tahini, dill, lemon juice, garlic, salt, pepper to taste, and reserved beet cooking juice until smooth. Transfer to a bowl. Serve at room temperature.

Feta-Spiked Edamame Dip with Arugula (page 51) and
Roasted Pepper and Sweet Potato Dip (page 16)

Sumptuous Spinach and Artichoke Dip (page 42)

Feta and Roasted Red Pepper Dip (page 48) and Tonnato (page 77)

Tzatziki (page 54)

Tuna Tapenade (page 78)

Nippy Oyster and Bacon Dip (page 80)
with Crisp Potato Wedges (page 27)

Fresh Tomato Salsa (page 86)

Asparagus Salsa (page 100)
on Basic Crostini (page 176)

Roasted Zucchini Dip

It's incredible what happens to zucchini when its roasted. Then you add sour cream and yum! Serve with crudités, such as carrot or celery sticks.

Makes about 1¼ cups (300 mL)

Tip

We prefer to use full-fat sour cream in this recipe because it has a deeper flavor profile but if you prefer, use a lower-fat alternative.

- **Preheat oven to 350°F (180°C)**
- **Food processor**

1½ cups	coarsely chopped zucchini	375 mL
¼ cup	extra virgin olive oil	60 mL
¼ tsp	salt	1 mL
¼ tsp	freshly ground black pepper	1 mL
½ cup	sour cream (see Tip, left)	125 mL
1 tbsp	freshly squeezed lemon juice	15 mL
1 tsp	minced rinsed capers	5 mL

1. On a rimmed baking sheet, combine zucchini, oil, salt and pepper and mix well to coat. Roast in preheated oven until soft, about 15 minutes.

2. Transfer mixture to a food processor fitted with metal blade and pulse until smooth. Transfer to a bowl and add sour cream, lemon juice and capers and mix well to combine. Serve immediately or cover and refrigerate for up to 3 days.

Dairy Dips and Spreads

Springtime Avocado Cream Cheese Dip

If you live in northern climates, this is a great dip to make in spring when the first spring onions and parsley start coming into markets. The ease of preparation and refreshing flavors will remind you of how delicious summer is going to be.

Makes about 2½ cups (625 mL)

Tips

We prefer to use Hass avocados, which are extremely creamy and flavorful. They are also inclined to be small. If your avocados are on the small side, consider using 3 in this recipe.

Dip keeps covered with plastic wrap and refrigerated for up to 4 hours.

• **Food processor**

8 oz	softened cream cheese, cut into cubes	250 g
6	green onions, white with a bit of green, cut into chunks	6
½ cup	fresh Italian flat-leaf parsley leaves	125 mL
¼ cup	freshly squeezed lemon juice	60 mL
2 tbsp	sour cream	30 mL
1	clove garlic, coarsely chopped	1
½ tsp	salt	2 mL
	Freshly ground black pepper	
2	large ripe avocados, cut into chunks (see Tips, left)	2

1. In food processor, process cream cheese, onions, parsley, lemon juice, sour cream, garlic and ½ tsp (2 mL) salt, until smooth. Add avocados and process until desired texture is achieved.

2. Transfer to a serving bowl. Season to taste with pepper. Serve immediately.

Black Pepper Goat Cheese Dip

Here's a very spicy, creamy treat for your palate that goes great with Basic Crostini (page 176) or Crisp Pita Bread (page 172).

Makes about 1½ cups (375 mL)

Tips

We prefer to use whole milk in this recipe because it has a deeper flavor profile but if you prefer, use a lower-fat version.

White balsamic vinegar is, like the regular version, cooked to intensify its flavor. But it is aged only for a short period and maintains its light color, which makes it useful in recipes where a darker color is not desirable.

⅔ cup	soft goat cheese (about 7 oz/210 g)	150 mL
½ cup	whole milk (see Tips, left)	125 mL
¼ cup	finely chopped cherry tomatoes	60 mL
2 tbsp	thinly sliced green onions	30 mL
1 tbsp	minced garlic	15 mL
1 tsp	freshly ground black pepper	5 mL
1 tsp	white balsamic vinegar (see Tips, left)	5 mL

1. In a bowl, mash together goat cheese and milk until smooth. Fold in tomatoes, green onions, garlic, pepper and vinegar until combined. Serve immediately or cover and refrigerate for up to 3 days.

Arugula-Spiked Goat Cheese

Use this as a spread or dip. It is terrifically easy to make and very tasty. It's refreshing and summery — a perfect addition to a garden party. Double or triple the quantity to suit your needs. Serve it with sliced baguette or crudités of seasonal vegetables.

Makes about 1 cup (250 mL)

Tips

Because this dip contains a significant quantity of fresh greens, which are likely to become soggy, we don't recommend storing it for longer than overnight.

When serving cold dips, particularly those that contain a high proportion of dairy, consider lining a deep platter with crushed ice and use it to surround the bowl. Arranging crudités over the ice will help to keep them nicely chilled as well.

• Food Processor

2 cups	packed baby arugula	500 mL
½ cup	packed Italian flat-leaf parsley leaves	125 mL
½	small red onion, halved	½
1	clove garlic, quartered	1
4 oz	soft goat cheese	125 g
1 tsp	grated lemon zest	5 mL
2 tbsp	freshly squeezed lemon juice	30 mL
2 tbsp	extra virgin olive oil	30 mL
½ tsp	salt	2 mL
	Freshly ground black pepper	

1. In food processor fitted with metal blade, pulse arugula, parsley, red onion and garlic until finely chopped, about 10 times. Add goat cheese, lemon zest and juice, olive oil, salt, and pepper to taste and process until blended, about 15 seconds. Cover and refrigerate until thoroughly chilled, for at least 2 hours.

Caramelized Onion Dip

This dip is one of life's guilty pleasures. Serve it with good potato chips (or, if you are ambitious, make your own; see page 165) and you'll be amazed: It will disappear to the very last drop.

Makes about 1½ cups (375 mL)

Tips

If you have problems digesting gluten, use brown rice miso, which is gluten-free.

The amount of salt you'll need to add depends upon the accompaniment. If you're serving this with salty potato chips, err on the side of caution.

- **Small (approx. 2 quart) slow cooker**
- **Food processor**

2	onions, thinly sliced on the vertical	2
4	cloves garlic, chopped	4
1 tbsp	melted butter	15 mL
4 oz	cream cheese, cubed and softened	125 g
½ cup	sour cream	125 mL
1 tbsp	dark miso (see Tips, left)	15 mL
	Salt and freshly ground black pepper (see Tips, left)	
	Finely snipped chives	
	Natural potato chips, optional	
	Belgian endive, optional	

1. In slow cooker stoneware, combine onions, garlic and butter. Toss well to ensure onions are thoroughly coated. Place a clean tea towel, folded in half (so you will have two layers), over top of stoneware to absorb moisture. Cover and cook on High for 5 hours, stirring two or three times to ensure onions are browning evenly, replacing towel each time, until onions are nicely caramelized.

2. Transfer mixture to food processor fitted with a metal blade. Add cream cheese, sour cream, miso, and salt and black pepper to taste. Process until well blended. Transfer to a serving dish and garnish with chives. Serve with potato chips or leaves of Belgian endive, if using.

Variation

For a more herbal flavor, add 2 tbsp (30 mL) fresh thyme leaves along with the cream cheese.

Caramelized
Red Onion Dip

Gone are the days when onion dip invariably involved a package of dried soup. Full of sweet red onions, this tasty alternative is very easy to make and the results are more than worth the extra effort. Serve with good-quality packaged potato chips, Homemade Potato Chips (page 165) or, for a more healthful option, spears of Belgian endive.

Makes about 2 cups (500 mL)

Tips

If you have a small (approx. 2 quart) slow cooker, it is a very convenient tool for caramelizing onions. For instructions, see Step 1, page 39.

You can caramelize the onions up to 2 days ahead of time and refrigerate until ready to use. Reheat gently before continuing with the recipe.

• **Food processor**

4	red onions, quartered	4
4	cloves garlic	4
2 tbsp	unsalted butter	30 mL
4 oz	cream cheese, cubed and softened	125 g
1/2 cup	sour cream	125 mL
2 tbsp	vegan or regular Worcestershire sauce	30 mL
2 tbsp	fresh thyme leaves	30 mL
	Salt and freshly ground black pepper	
	Finely snipped chives	

1. In food processor fitted with slicing blade, slice red onions and garlic.

2. In a large skillet, melt butter over medium heat. Add red onions and garlic and stir well. Cook, stirring, until onions are browned and caramelized, about 25 minutes (see Tips, left).

3. Replace slicing blade with metal blade. Add caramelized onion mixture, cream cheese, sour cream, Worcestershire sauce, thyme, and salt and pepper to taste, to food processor. Process until well blended, about 30 seconds. Transfer to a serving dish and garnish with chives.

Smoky Baked Onion Dip

On those days when you feel like throwing caution to the wind, open a bag of good potato chips and serve up a batch of this luscious dip — one of life's little indulgences. It is also good with melba toast or sliced baguette.

Makes about 2 cups (500 mL)

Tips

If you have an ovenproof serving dish of the appropriate size, by all means use it to make this dish.

Smoked paprika has great flavor but it can be overpowering. Add the smaller quantity and taste. If you prefer stronger flavor add the remainder.

- **Preheat oven to 400°F (200°C)**
- **Lightly greased baking dish (see Tips, left)**

1	large Spanish onion (about 12 oz/375 g), finely chopped	1
1 tbsp	olive oil	15 mL
1½ cups	shredded Swiss cheese	375 mL
8 oz	cream cheese, softened	250 g
½ cup	freshly grated Parmesan cheese, divided	125 mL
¼ cup	mayonnaise	60 mL
1 tbsp	vegan or regular Worcestershire sauce	15 mL
½ to 1 tsp	hot smoked paprika (see Tips, left)	2 to 5 mL
	Salt and freshly ground black pepper	

1. In a microwave-safe bowl large enough to accommodate all the ingredients, combine onion and oil. Cover and microwave on High for 2 minutes. Stir well. Add Swiss cheese, cream cheese, ¼ cup (60 mL) of the Parmesan, mayonnaise, Worcestershire sauce, paprika and salt and pepper to taste. Mix well. Transfer to prepared dish. Sprinkle remaining Parmesan evenly over top.

2. Bake in preheated oven until mixture is bubbling and top is lightly browned, about 25 minutes. Serve immediately.

Sumptuous Spinach and Artichoke Dip

Spinach and artichoke dip has become a classic. Serve with toast points, Basic Crostini (page 176), tostadas or tortilla chips, or sliced baguette.

Makes 6 to 8 servings

Tips

If you are using fresh spinach leaves in this recipe, take care to wash them thoroughly, as they can be quite gritty. *To wash spinach:* Fill a clean sink with lukewarm water. Remove the tough stems and submerge the tender leaves in the water, swishing to remove the grit. Rinse thoroughly in a colander under cold running water, checking carefully to ensure that no sand remains. If you are using frozen spinach in this recipe, thaw and squeeze the excess moisture out before adding to the slow cooker.

If you prefer a smoother dip, place spinach and artichokes in a food processor, in separate batches, and pulse until desired degree of fineness is achieved. Then combine with remaining ingredients in slow cooker stoneware.

- **Small (maximum 3½ quart) slow cooker**

1 cup	shredded mozzarella cheese	250 mL
8 oz	cream cheese, cubed	250 g
¼ cup	freshly grated Parmesan cheese	60 mL
1	clove garlic, minced	1
¼ tsp	freshly ground black pepper	1 mL
1	can (14 oz/398 mL) artichokes, drained and finely chopped	1
1 lb	fresh spinach, stems removed, or 1 package (10 oz/300 g) spinach leaves, thawed if frozen (see Tips, left)	500 g

1. In slow cooker stoneware, combine cheese, cream cheese, Parmesan, garlic, pepper, artichokes and spinach. Cover and cook on High for 2 hours, until hot and bubbly. Stir well and serve.

Classic Spinach and Water Chestnut Dip

Versions of this dip have been around for decades but it just doesn't go away — probably because it qualifies as comfort food. It's great with traditional crudités, such as celery sticks, warm pita, toast points, sliced baguette, or chunks of sourdough bread.

Makes about 2 cups (500 mL)

Tips

To clean leeks: Fill a sink full of lukewarm water. Split the leeks in half lengthwise and submerge them in the water, swishing them around to remove all traces of dirt. Transfer to a colander and rinse thoroughly under cold water.

For this quantity of spinach leaves, use a 1 lb (500 g) bunch of fresh spinach. Remove the stems and discard.

Use the kind of red or green chile you have easy access to. Long red or Thai bird's eye both work well in this recipe. If you're heat averse, seed and devein the chile before using.

For this quantity of water chestnuts, use about two-thirds of an 8-oz (227 g) can, drained.

● **Food processor**

2 tbsp	unsalted butter	30 mL
1	leek, white and light green part only, cleaned and thinly sliced (see Tips, left)	1
2	cloves garlic, chopped	2
10 oz	fresh spinach leaves (see Tips, left)	300 g
2 tsp	grainy Dijon mustard	10 mL
1/4 to 1/2	long red or green chile pepper (see Tips, left)	1/4 to 1/2
4 oz	cream cheese, softened	125 g
1/4 cup	sour cream	60 mL
1/2 cup	sliced water chestnuts (see Tips, left)	125 mL
	Salt and freshly ground black pepper	

1. In a skillet, melt butter over medium heat. Add leek and cook, stirring, until softened, about 5 minutes. Add garlic and cook, stirring, for 1 minute. Add spinach and toss until wilted, about 2 minutes. Remove from heat and stir in mustard and chile pepper to taste.

2. Transfer to food processor fitted with metal blade. Add cream cheese, sour cream and water chestnuts and process until smooth, about 1 minute. Transfer to a serving bowl. Season to taste with salt and pepper.

Cilantro Lime Dip

Use this dip to complete a southwestern-themed party. Serve with tortilla chips for dipping or use it as a topping for quesadillas.

Makes about 1¼ cups (300 mL)

Tips

We prefer to use full-fat or whole milk yogurt in this recipe because it has a deeper flavor profile but if you prefer, use a lower-fat alternative.

For best flavor, toast and grind cumin yourself. *To toast seeds:* Place seeds in a dry skillet over medium heat and cook, stirring, until fragrant about 3 minutes. Immediately transfer to a mortar or a spice grinder and grind.

½ cup	coarsely chopped fresh cilantro leaves	125 mL
½ cup	plain yogurt (see Tips, left)	125 mL
¼ cup	freshly squeezed lime juice	60 mL
2 tbsp	cream cheese, softened	30 mL
¼ tsp	ground cumin (see Tips, left)	1 mL
⅛ tsp	salt	0.5 mL

1. In a bowl, combine cilantro, yogurt, lime juice, cream cheese, cumin and salt until smooth. Serve immediately or cover and refrigerate for up to 3 days.

Cucumber Cottage Cheese Dip

This refreshing dip is light and tasty. It's ideal for guests who are trying to gain control of their waistlines, but others will enjoy it, too. Serve with crudités or crackers.

Makes about 1¼ cups (300 mL)

Tip

Using pressed dry cottage cheese produces a dip that is substantial enough to adhere to veggie dippers.

• **Food processor**

½ cup	unsalted dry pressed cottage cheese (about 8 oz/250 g) (see Tip, left)	125 mL
1 tbsp	mayonnaise	15 mL
½	English cucumber, peeled, seeded and cut into chunks	½
4	green onions, white part with a bit of green, cut into chunks	4
2 tbsp	fresh dill fronds, optional	30 mL
	Salt and freshly ground black pepper	

1. In food processor fitted with metal blade, process cottage cheese and mayonnaise until smooth and light. Add cucumber, green onions, and dill, if using, and pulse until chopped and blended. Season to taste with salt and pepper.

2. Transfer to a serving bowl or cover and refrigerate for up to 3 days.

Dill Cucumber Dip

This is fantastic as a dip with pita bread or fresh cut cucumbers. It's also the ultimate garnish to gravlax.

Makes about 1½ cups (375 mL)

Tip

When serving cold dips, particularly those that contain a high proportion of dairy, consider lining a deep platter with crushed ice and use it to surround the bowl. Arranging crudités over the ice will help to keep them nicely chilled as well.

1¼ cups	sour cream (see Tip, left)	300 mL
½ cup	grated English cucumber	125 mL
¼ cup	coarsely chopped fresh dill fronds	60 mL
1 tsp	grated lemon zest	5 mL
1 tsp	white balsamic or apple cider vinegar	5 mL
½ tsp	salt	2 mL
⅛ tsp	freshly ground black pepper	0.5 mL

1. In a bowl, combine sour cream, cucumber, dill, lemon zest, vinegar, salt and pepper. Cover with a tight-fitting lid and refrigerate for 1 day before serving or for up to 3 days. Stir well before serving.

Variation

If you like mint, feel free to replace the dill with mint in this recipe.

Lemon Garlic Dip

Vegetarian Friendly

This all-purpose dip has an appealing lemon flavor that makes a perfect finish for crudités. It also makes an excellent spread on sandwiches.

Makes about 1½ cups (375 mL)		
¾ cup	sour cream	175 mL
⅓ cup	dry pressed cottage cheese (see Tip, page 45)	75 mL
¼ cup	freshly squeezed lemon juice	60 mL
1 tbsp	minced garlic (see Tip, left)	15 mL
1 tbsp	thinly sliced green onions	15 mL

Tip

Convenience products are available everywhere and we encourage their use on one condition — no preservatives. Don't shy away from great-quality frozen products such as puréed garlic.

1. In a bowl, combine sour cream, cottage cheese, lemon juice, garlic and green onions until smooth. Serve immediately or cover and refrigerate for up to 3 days.

Feta and Roasted Red Pepper Dip

If you have the ingredients on hand, this tasty dip can be ready to serve in about 5 minutes. Serve it with crudités, crackers or pumpernickel rounds for an elegant appetizer.

Makes about 1¾ cups (425 mL)

Tip

Use creamy feta cheese (about 26% M.F.). The lower-fat versions produce a drier dip. If your results seem dry, add 1 tsp (5 mL) or so of extra virgin olive oil and pulse.

• Food processor

8 oz	feta cheese (see Tip, left)	250 g
2	roasted red bell peppers, quartered (see Tips, page 30) or store-bought	2
	Hot pepper sauce, optional	

1. In food processor fitted with metal blade, process feta, roasted peppers, and hot pepper sauce, if using, until smooth, about 30 seconds, stopping and scraping down sides of the bowl as necessary.

2. Transfer to a bowl and serve or cover and refrigerate for up to 3 days. If refrigerated allow to stand at room temperature for 20 minutes before serving.

Feta and Yogurt Dip

Nothing could be simpler to make than this herb-infused spread. A small bowl of olives makes a nice accompaniment. Serve with Crisp Pita Bread (page 172), warm pita, crackers or crudités.

Makes about 1 cup (250 mL)

Tip

Make an effort to get Greek-style yogurt, also known as "pressed." It is lusciously thick and adds beautiful depth to this and many other dishes. If you can't find Greek yogurt, you can make your own. *To make Greek-Style yogurt:* Line a sieve with a double layer of cheesecloth or paper towels. Add plain yogurt, cover and refrigerate overnight. The watery component will have drained out and you will be be left with lovely thick yogurt.

- **Food processor**

1 cup	crumbled feta cheese (about 8 oz/250 g)	250 mL
1 cup	plain yogurt, preferably Greek-style (pressed) (see Tip, left)	250 mL
½ cup	fresh dill fronds	125 mL
½ cup	snipped chives	125 mL
	Freshly ground black pepper	
	Extra virgin olive oil	

1. In food processor fitted with metal blade, process feta, yogurt, dill, chives, and pepper to taste until smooth, about 30 seconds. Transfer to a serving bowl and drizzle with olive oil.

Feta Cucumber Dip

A refreshing creamy dip that is wonderful with warm breads, Crisp Pita Bread or any of its seasoned variations (page 172).

Makes about 1½ cups (375 mL)

Tip

We prefer to use full-fat or whole milk yogurt in this recipe because it has a deeper flavor profile but if you prefer, use a lower-fat alternative. The same holds true for sour cream.

¾ cup	plain yogurt (see Tip, left)	175 mL
½ cup	crumbled feta cheese	125 mL
½ cup	grated English cucumber	125 mL
1 tsp	finely chopped fresh thyme leaves	5 mL

1. In a bowl, combine yogurt, feta, cucumber and thyme until smooth. Serve immediately or cover and refrigerate for up to 3 days.

Variation

Combine ¼ cup (60 mL) Feta Cucumber Dip with 2 tbsp (30 mL) red wine vinegar and ½ cup (125 mL) each chopped cucumbers, large chopped tomatoes and kalamata olives for a lovely quick Greek Salad.

Feta-Spiked Edamame Dip with Arugula

Healthful and refreshing, this delicious dip is also visually attractive — it's an extremely pretty shade of green. It's great with pita bread, tortilla chips, cucumber slices and celery sticks.

Makes about 2 cups (500 mL)

Tip

Because this dip contains arugula, which will become soggy, we don't recommend storing it for longer than overnight.

- **Food processor**

2 cups	frozen shelled edamame beans, thawed	500 mL
4 cups	packed baby arugula leaves	1 L
2	green onions, white part with a bit of green, cut into chunks	2
½ cup	crumbled feta cheese (about 3 oz/90 g)	125 mL
¼ cup	extra virgin olive oil	60 mL
2 tbsp	freshly squeezed lemon juice	30 mL
	Salt and freshly ground black pepper	

1. In a pot of boiling salted water, boil edamame beans until tender, about 2 minutes. Scoop off 1 cup (250 mL) of the cooking liquid and set aside. Drain beans and transfer to food processor. Add arugula and green onions and pulse until coarsely chopped.

2. Add feta, oil, lemon juice and salt and pepper to taste and process until smooth, about 1 minute. With motor running, add enough cooking liquid to make a smooth purée. Transfer to a serving bowl. Serve immediately.

Spiced Feta

Feta is to some cultures what Philadelphia cream cheese is to North Americans: a *tabula rasa* upon which to build an infinite number of delicious combinations. Here garden-fresh ingredients and a splash of extra virgin olive oil transform the pleasantly salty cheese into a tasty dip. Serve with warm pita or crudités such as sliced cucumber.

Makes about 2 cups (500 mL)

Tips

If you prefer, use chopped cherry tomatoes.

If you don't like heat, seed the chile and remove the veins.

• **Food processor**

8 oz	feta cheese, crumbled	250 g
1 cup	chopped tomato (see Tips, left)	250 mL
6	green onions, white part with a bit of green, chopped	6
1	long red chile pepper, chopped (see Tips, left)	1
2 tbsp	extra virgin olive oil	30 mL
2 tbsp	fresh dill fronds	30 mL
1 tbsp	freshly squeezed lemon juice	15 mL
	Salt and freshly ground black pepper	

1. In food processor fitted with metal blade, process feta, tomato, green onions, chile pepper, oil, dill and lemon juice until smooth, about 1 minute, stopping and scraping down sides of the bowl as necessary. Season to taste with salt and black pepper. Transfer to a serving bowl and refrigerate until ready to serve.

Greek Salad Dip

Serve this dip with warm pita bread or Crisp Pita Bread (page 172). If you're looking for a showstopper presentation, hollow out a whole rye bread and fill the cavity with Greek Salad Dip. Tear the rye "flesh" into large two-bite pieces and use that as the dipper...it's yummy!

Makes about 1¾ cups (425 mL)

Tip

When serving cold dips, particularly those that contain a high proportion of dairy, consider lining a deep platter with crushed ice and use it to surround the bowl. Arranging crudités over the ice will help to keep them nicely chilled as well.

1 cup	crumbled feta cheese	250 mL
½ cup	heavy or whipping (35%) cream	125 mL
½ cup	grated English cucumber	125 mL
½ cup	finely chopped ripe tomato	125 mL
1 tbsp	grated red onion	15 mL
1 tbsp	minced kalamata olives	15 mL

1. In a bowl, mash together feta and cream until smooth. Fold in cucumber, tomato, red onion and olives. Cover and refrigerate overnight before serving.

Variation

Add ¼ cup (60 mL) Champagne vinegar or white wine vinegar to this recipe to create a wonderful vinaigrette suitable for any salad but specifically great on a Greek one.

Tzatziki

This classic Greek condiment is a great dip with warm pita, Crisp Pita Bread (page 172) or crudités. It also makes a great dipping sauce for souvlakis.

Makes about 2½ cups (625 mL)

Tips

Be sure to seed your cucumber. Otherwise your tzatziki is likely to be watery.

We always use flat-leaf rather than curly parsley because it has more flavor.

When serving cold dips, particularly those that contain a high proportion of dairy, consider lining a deep platter with crushed ice and use it to surround the bowl. Arranging crudités over the ice will help to keep them nicely chilled as well.

• **Food processor**

2 cups	plain Greek-style (pressed) yogurt (see Tip, page 49)	500 mL
1	cucumber, peeled, seeded and cut into chunks (see Tips, left)	1
½ cup	loosely packed Italian flat-leaf parsley leaves or fresh dill fronds	125 mL
2	cloves garlic, coarsely chopped	2
2 tbsp	extra virgin olive oil	30 mL
2 tbsp	freshly squeezed lemon juice	30 mL
1 tsp	salt	5 mL

1. In food processor fitted with metal blade, process yogurt, cucumber, parsley, garlic, olive oil, lemon juice and salt until smooth.

2. Transfer to a serving bowl. Cover and refrigerate until chilled or for up to 3 days.

Pommery Mustard Dip

Use as a dip for crudités — but remember, no double dipping! This also makes a nice garnish for burgers.

Makes about 1½ cups (375 mL)

Tip

Pommery or stone-ground mustard is made from spices, vinegar and whole mustard seeds and is widely used in France. Although we like its grainy texture in this recipe, a classic Dijon would work well in its place.

1 cup	crème fraîche	250 mL
¼ cup	grainy (Pommery) mustard (see Tip, left)	60 mL
¼ cup	ricotta cheese	60 mL
1 tbsp	soft goat cheese	15 mL
1 tsp	finely chopped fresh thyme leaves	5 mL
½ tsp	hot pepper flakes	2 mL
½ tsp	Champagne vinegar or white wine vinegar	2 mL
¼ tsp	salt	1 mL
¼ tsp	freshly ground black pepper	1 mL

1. In a bowl, combine crème fraîche, mustard, ricotta, goat cheese, thyme, hot pepper flakes, vinegar, salt and pepper until smooth. Serve immediately or cover and refrigerate for up to 3 days. Bring dip to room temperature before serving.

Roasted Beet and Goat Cheese Spread

Vegetarian Friendly

This spread is amazing with sliders, Basic Crostini (page 176), or Crisp Pita Bread (page 172).

Makes about 1½ cups (375 mL)

Tip

When serving cold dips, particularly those that contain a high proportion of dairy, consider lining a deep platter with crushed ice and use it to surround the bowl. Arranging crudités over the ice will help to keep them nicely chilled as well.

- **Preheat oven to 400°F (200°C)**
- **Food processor**

2	medium beets, scrubbed	2
	Olive oil	
1 tsp	fresh dill fronds	5 mL
½ cup	soft goat cheese, at room temperature	125 mL
½ cup	sour cream (see Tip, left)	125 mL

1. Place beets on a rimmed baking sheet or in a baking dish. Toss with oil and cover with foil. Roast in preheated oven until tender, about 1 hour. Remove from oven. Let beets cool, then using a piece of paper towel, rub off skins. Coarsely chop. (You should have ¾ cup/175 mL.)

2. In food processor fitted with metal blade, purée beets and dill until smooth.

3. In a bowl, mash together goat cheese and sour cream until smooth. Stir in beet purée. Serve immediately or cover and refrigerate for up to 3 days.

Roasted Carrot and Yogurt Dip

If you're looking for a slightly different but delicious taste sensation, try this Middle Eastern–inspired dip. It's perfect on Crisp Pita Bread (page 172) but if you want to go the extra mile, try enhancing the regional flavors with Crisp Pita Bread with Dukkah (see Variations, page 173).

Makes about 1½ cups (375 mL)

Tip

For best flavor, toast and grind cumin yourself.
To toast seeds: Place seeds in a dry skillet over medium heat and cook, stirring, until fragrant, about 3 minutes. Immediately transfer to a mortar or spice grinder and grind.

- **Preheat oven to 425°F (220°C)**
- **Food processor**

8	carrots, peeled and cut into chunks	8
2 tbsp	olive oil	30 mL
2	cloves garlic, minced	2
2 tsp	ground cumin (see Tip, left)	10 mL
1 tsp	ground coriander	5 mL
1 tbsp	harissa	15 mL
¾ cup	plain Greek-style (pressed) yogurt (see Tip, page 49)	175 mL
	Finely chopped parsley	

1. In a bowl, combine carrots and oil. Transfer to a baking sheet and roast in preheated oven, turning, until soft, about 45 minutes. Let cool.

2. In food processor, pulse carrots, garlic, cumin, coriander and harissa until coarsely chopped. Add yogurt and pulse until blended. Spoon into a bowl and garnish with parsley. Serve warm.

Roasted Garlic Sour Cream Dip

It's amazing how sweet garlic can become when roasted. Serve with Homemade Potato Chips (page 165) or Salt-Roasted Potatoes (page 162).

Makes about 1½ cups (375 mL)

Tip

We prefer to use full-fat or whole milk yogurt and sour cream in this recipe because it has a deeper flavor profile but if you prefer, use a lower-fat alternative.

- **Preheat oven to 400°F (200°C)**

2	bulbs garlic	2
2 tbsp	extra virgin olive oil	30 mL
¼ tsp	salt	1 mL
½ cup	plain yogurt (see Tip, left)	125 mL
½ cup	sour cream	125 mL
1 tsp	finely chopped chives	5 mL

1. Cut whole garlic bulbs in half along their "equator" and thoroughly coat with olive oil. Combine the two halves and wrap in foil. Roast in preheated oven until bulbs are soft, about 1 hour. Let cool to room temperature. Squeeze garlic out of skins into a bowl to release caramelized cloves. Sprinkle with salt.

2. In a bowl, combine ½ cup (125 mL) roasted garlic, yogurt, sour cream and chives. Cover and refrigerate overnight to allow flavors to meld or for up to 3 days.

Homemade Herb Cheese

In the tradition of simple cheese spreads, this is easy to make yet delicious. Serve this flavorful cheese with breadsticks or celery sticks, or on sliced baguette or crackers.

Makes about ¾ cup (175 mL)

Tip

When serving cold dips, particularly those that contain a high proportion of dairy, consider lining a deep platter with crushed ice and use it to surround the bowl. Arranging crudités over the ice will help to keep them nicely chilled as well.

- **Food processor**

¼ cup	crème fraîche	60 mL
2 tbsp	chopped parsley leaves	30 mL
2 tbsp	snipped chives	30 mL
2	cloves garlic, coarsely chopped	2
1 tsp	cracked black peppercorns	5 mL
4 oz	soft goat cheese	125 g

1. In food processor fitted with metal blade, process crème fraîche, parsley, chives, garlic and peppercorns until smoothly blended, stopping and scraping down sides of the bowl as necessary. Add goat cheese and process until smooth, about 30 seconds.

Liptauer

This is a classic Austrian/Hungarian dish, often made with Camembert, combined with a creamy cottage cheese. Here it's made with cream cheese and Emmental with lively additions such as hot smoked paprika. It is delicious served with thin slices of dark rye bread.

Makes about 1 cup (250 mL)

Tip

Don't confuse real mayonnaise with "mayonnaise-type" salad dressings, which are similar in appearance. Mayonnaise is a combination of egg yolks, vinegar or lemon juice, olive oil and seasonings. Imitators will contain additional ingredients, such as sugar, flour or milk. Make your own or make sure the label says mayonnaise and check the ingredients.

• Food processor

4 oz	Swiss Emmental cheese, shredded	125 g
4 oz	cream cheese, cubed and softened	125 g
¼ cup	mayonnaise (see Tip, left)	60 mL
1 tbsp	Dijon mustard	15 mL
1	shallot, coarsely chopped	1
2	cornichon or gherkin pickles	2
1 tbsp	drained capers	15 mL
2 tsp	caraway seeds	10 mL
½ tsp	hot smoked paprika	2 mL
	Freshly ground black pepper	

1. In food processor fitted with metal blade, process Swiss cheese, cream cheese, mayonnaise, Dijon mustard, shallot, cornichons, capers, caraway and paprika until smoothly blended, about 20 seconds. Season to taste with pepper.

Pimento Cheese

Pimento cheese is an old favorite in the southern U.S. Serve this with sliced baguette, crackers, cracker bread or celery sticks.

Makes about
1½ cups (375 mL)

Tip

If you prefer, substitute ¼ cup (60 mL) coarsely chopped sweet onion, such as Vidalia, for the green or red.

• **Food processor**

8 oz	sharp (aged) Cheddar cheese	250 g
1	roasted red bell pepper (see Tips, page 30)	1
½ cup	mayonnaise	125 mL
3 tbsp	chopped green or red onion (see Tip, left)	45 mL
	Hot pepper sauce	
	Freshly ground black pepper	

1. In food processor fitted with shredding blade, shred Cheddar. Replace shredding blade with metal blade. Add roasted pepper, mayonnaise, onion, and hot pepper sauce and black pepper to taste, and pulse until onion is finely chopped and mixture is blended, about 10 times.

2. Transfer to a small serving bowl or earthenware crock, cover and refrigerate for at least 2 hours or for up to 2 days. Before serving let stand at room temperature to allow the flavors to bloom, about 20 minutes.

Kentucky Beer Cheese

In Kentucky, this spread is an indigenous treat — some call it America's answer to Britain's Welsh rarebit. Serve with sliced baguette, rye bread or celery sticks. Or spread it on toast, garnish with sliced tomatoes and run under the broiler for a delicious lunch.

Makes about 2½ cups (625 mL)

Tips

If you have a mini-bowl attachment, it is ideal for this recipe.

Use light or dark beer to suit your preference.

• **Food processor (see Tips, left)**

8 oz	extra sharp (aged) Cheddar, cubed	250 g
8 oz	Monterey Jack, cubed	250 g
¾ cup	beer, divided (see Tips, left)	175 mL
2	cloves garlic, coarsely chopped	2
2 tbsp	coarsely snipped chives	30 mL
1 tbsp	vegan or regular Worcestershire sauce	15 mL
1 tbsp	Dijon mustard	15 mL
	Hot pepper sauce	
	Freshly ground black pepper	
	Paprika	

1. In food processor, process Cheddar and Monterey Jack cheeses, ¼ cup (60 mL) of the beer, garlic, chives, Worcestershire, mustard, and pepper sauce and pepper to taste until combined. Add remaining beer and process until smooth.

2. Spoon into a serving bowl, cover and refrigerate for at least 2 hours. Dust with paprika before serving.

Cheddar Cheese Fondue

This silky cheesy dip is great for bread and vegetables. It's particularly good with broccoli and cauliflower florets as dippers. You could also try it as the new "cheese" for your burgers or on the side. Try it — you and your guests will love it.

Makes
2 cups (500 mL)

Tip

We prefer to use whole milk in this recipe because it has a deeper flavor profile but if you prefer, use a lower-fat alternative.

1 tbsp	unsalted butter	15 mL
3 tbsp	all-purpose flour (see Tip, below)	45 mL
1½ cups	whole milk (see Tip, left)	375 mL
2 cups	shredded Cheddar cheese	500 mL
1 tsp	finely chopped fresh chives	5 mL

1. In a saucepan, melt butter over medium-low heat. Sprinkle with flour and cook, stirring often, until smooth and a nutty brown color, 4 to 5 minutes. Gradually whisk in milk. Cook, stirring, until bubbling and thickened, about 5 minutes. Remove from heat and slowly add cheese, about 1 tbsp (15 mL) at a time, whisking to incorporate. Transfer to a serving dish. Garnish with chives and serve immediately.

Blue Cheese Fondue

This tart fondue is perfect with everything from simple carrot sticks to Buffalo chicken wings.

Makes
2 cup (500 mL)

Tip

If you have trouble digesting gluten, substitute an equal quality of all-purpose gluten-free flour for the regular version.

1 tbsp	unsalted butter	15 mL
3 tbsp	all-purpose flour (see Tip, left)	45 mL
1½ cups	whole milk	375 mL
8 oz	crumbled loosely packed blue cheese	250 g
1 tsp	finely grated toasted pecans	5 mL

1. In a saucepan, melt butter over medium-low heat. Sprinkle with flour and cook, stirring often, until smooth and a nutty brown color, 4 to 5 minutes. Gradually whisk in milk. Cook, stirring, until bubbling and thickened, about 5 minutes Remove from heat and add cheese, about 1 tbsp (15 mL) at a time, and whisk to incorporate. Repeat until all cheese has been added. Garnish with pecans and serve immediately.

Fish, Seafood and Meat Dips and Spreads

Anchovy-Spiked Avocado Dip

If you're a fan of guacamole, but would enjoy a slightly different flavor profile, try this. Although avocados and anchovies may not seem like an obvious pairing, they complement each other surprisingly well. Serve with tostadas or tortilla chips.

Makes about 2 cups (500 mL)

Tip

We prefer to use Hass avocados, which are extremely creamy and flavorful.

• **Food processor**

3	small avocados, such as Hass, cut into chunks (see Tip, left)	3
8	cherry tomatoes	8
6	green onions, white part with a bit of green, cut into chunks	6
4	anchovy fillets	4
1/4 cup	sour cream	60 mL
2 tbsp	freshly squeezed lemon juice	30 mL
	Salt and freshly ground black pepper	

1. In food processor fitted with metal blade, process avocados, tomatoes, green onions, anchovies, sour cream and lemon juice until desired texture is achieved. Season to taste with salt and pepper.

2. Transfer to a serving bowl. Serve immediately or cover with plastic wrap, pressing down on surface of dip, and refrigerate for up to 4 hours.

Anchoyade de Croze

This unusual but delicious spread is named after the French cookbook author Austin de Croze, who invented it. It is traditionally spread on country bread brushed with olive oil and baked, a form of bruschetta, but warm crostini or even sliced baguette work well, too.

Tips

Use the chile pepper of your choice. We have also made this using 1½ tbsp (22 mL) drained chopped hot pickled banana peppers, which produces a very nice result.

Orange blossom water is available in specialty stores and Middle Eastern markets. It is very strongly flavored. This quantity produces a nice result, but if you like the taste, add a bit more after the ingredients have been combined and pulse to blend.

- **Food processor**

4	dried figs	4
1	can (2 oz/60 g) anchovy fillets, drained (about 12)	1
12	blanched almonds (see Tips, page 15)	12
2	cloves garlic	2
1	small red onion, quartered	1
1	roasted red bell pepper (see Tips, page 70)	1
1	bottled chile pepper (see Tips, left)	1
¼ cup	fresh Italian flat-leaf parsley leaves	60 mL
¼ cup	fresh tarragon leaves	60 mL
2 tbsp	freshly squeezed lemon juice	30 mL
½ tsp	fennel seeds, crushed	2 mL
¼ cup	extra virgin olive oil (approx.)	60 mL
½ tsp	orange blossom water (see Tips, left)	2 mL
	Hot pepper sauce, optional	

1. In a bowl of warm water, soak figs until softened, about 15 minutes. Drain, remove tough stem ends and chop coarsely.

2. In food processor fitted with metal blade, pulse figs, anchovies, almonds, garlic, red onion, roasted pepper, chile pepper, parsley, tarragon, lemon juice and fennel several times to chop. With motor running, add olive oil through feed tube and process until a smooth paste is formed, about 1 minute. Add orange blossom water, and hot pepper sauce to taste, if using.

3. Transfer to a serving bowl. Cover and refrigerate for at least 2 hours or for up to 3 days.

Artichoke and Olive Tapenade

Here's a slightly different spin on tapenade. With the addition of artichokes, it's a bit lighter than the norm. It's delicious served on warm pita or Crisp Pita Bread (page 172).

(page 172).

Makes about 2 cups (500 mL)

Tips

We always use flat-leaf rather than curly parsley because it has more flavor.

For best results use nonpareil capers. They are the smallest version of the edible flower buds and they have the best flavor and most pleasing texture.

• **Food processor**

1	can (14 oz/398 mL) artichoke hearts, drained	1
½ cup	pitted black olives	125 mL
¼ cup	Italian flat-leaf parsley leaves (see Tips, left)	60 mL
2 tbsp	drained capers (see Tips, left)	30 mL
2 tbsp	freshly squeezed lemon juice	30 mL
2	anchovy fillets	2
2	cloves garlic	2
¼ cup	extra virgin olive oil	60 mL
	Salt and freshly ground black pepper	
	Paprika, optional	

1. In food processor fitted with metal blade, pulse artichokes, olives, parsley, capers, lemon juice, anchovies and garlic until finely chopped, about 10 times. Add olive oil and pulse to blend, about 5 times. Season to taste with salt and pepper.

2. Transfer to a serving bowl. Cover and refrigerate for at least 2 hours or for up to 1 day. Dust lightly with paprika, if using, before serving.

Parsley-Laced Tapenade with Roasted Pepper

The addition of parsley and a roasted red pepper adds lightness to tapenade, which tends to be heavy. Serve this on sliced baguette or celery sticks or as part of an antipasto table.

Makes about 1¼ cups (300 mL)

Tip

For best results, use olives from the Mediterranean region. Do not use canned black olives, which are completely lacking in taste.

• **Food processor**

8 oz	pitted drained black olives (see Tip, left)	250 g
2 tbsp	drained capers	30 mL
1 cup	loosely packed Italian flat-leaf parsley leaves	250 mL
2	anchovy fillets	2
1	clove garlic, coarsely chopped	1
1	roasted red bell pepper, coarsely chopped (see Tips, page 70)	1
¼ cup	extra virgin olive oil	60 mL

1. In food processor fitted with metal blade, pulse olives, capers, parsley, anchovies, garlic and roasted pepper until chopped and combined, about 10 times, stopping and scraping down sides of the bowl as necessary. Add olive oil and pulse until desired texture is achieved.

2. Transfer to a serving bowl. Serve immediately or cover and refrigerate for up to 3 days. If refrigerated, before serving, let stand at room temperature for about 20 minutes to allow the flavors to develop.

Easy Roasted Red Pepper Dip

Serve this when gorgeous red peppers are abundant in farmers' markets and relatively inexpensive. It's incredibly easy to make and delivers tremendous bang for the effort invested. It's great with thinly sliced baguette, warm pita bread or crudités.

Makes about 1½ cups (375 mL)

Tips

To roast peppers: Preheat broiler. Place peppers on a baking sheet and broil, turning two or three times, until skin on all sides is blackened, about 25 minutes. Transfer to a heatproof bowl. Cover with a plate and let stand until cool. Remove and, using a sharp knife, lift skins off. Discard skins, core and seeds.

For convenience, you can use store-bought roasted peppers.

• **Food processor**

2	roasted red bell peppers, quartered (see Tips, left)	2
¼ cup	mayonnaise	60 mL
2 tbsp	Italian flat-leaf parsley leaves	30 mL
1	anchovy fillet	1
1	clove garlic, coarsely chopped	1
2 tsp	extra virgin olive oil	10 mL
2 tsp	white wine vinegar flavored with tarragon	10 mL
2 tbsp	plain Greek-style (pressed) yogurt (see Tip, page 71)	30 mL
	Salt and freshly ground black pepper	

1. In food processor fitted with metal blade, process roasted peppers, mayonnaise, parsley, anchovy, garlic, olive oil and vinegar until smoothly puréed.

2. Transfer to a serving bowl and stir in yogurt. Season to taste with salt and pepper. Serve immediately or cover and refrigerate for up to 3 days.

Green Goddess Dipping Sauce

This is the perfect summer dip because it makes a fabulous partner for a wide variety of garden vegetables. Crisp hearts of romaine lettuce, small wedges of radicchio, sliced cucumber, radishes or cherry tomatoes all benefit from a brush with this tasty blend. If you're looking for something more substantial, consider cold cooked shrimp or crab claws.

Makes about 1½ cups (375 mL)

Tip

Make an effort to get Greek-style yogurt, also known as "pressed." It is lusciously thick and adds beautiful depth to this and many other dishes. If you can't find Greek yogurt, you can make your own. *To make Greek-Style yogurt:* Line a sieve with a double layer of cheesecloth or paper towels. Add plain yogurt, cover and refrigerate overnight. The watery component will have drained out and you will be be left with lovely thick yogurt.

• Food processor

½ cup	mayonnaise	125 mL
½ cup	plain Greek-style (pressed) yogurt (see Tip, left)	125 mL
½ cup	Italian flat-leaf parsley leaves	125 mL
¼ cup	snipped chives	60 mL
¼ cup	fresh tarragon leaves	60 mL
4	anchovy fillets	4
2 tbsp	freshly squeezed lemon juice	30 mL
1 tbsp	white wine or Champagne vinegar	15 mL
½ tsp	salt or to taste	2 mL
	Freshly ground black pepper	

1. In food processor fitted with metal blade, process mayonnaise, yogurt, parsley, chives, tarragon, anchovies, lemon juice, vinegar, salt, and pepper to taste until smooth. Taste and adjust seasoning. (You may want a bit more lemon juice and/or salt.)

2. Transfer to a serving bowl. Cover and refrigerate for at least 1 hour to allow flavors to meld.

Warm Anchovy Dip

To many the mere mention of an anchovy is a turn off but "melted" with Dijon mustard and served with crudités, this is one of the most special flavors ever. The French serve this dip with freshly cut carrots, button mushrooms, cauliflower or any other seasonal vegetable.

Makes about 1½ cups (375 mL)

1 cup	roughly chopped anchovy fillets	250 mL
⅓ cup	extra virgin olive oil	75 mL
1 tsp	Dijon mustard	5 mL
1 tsp	minced garlic	5 mL
1 tsp	liquid honey	5 mL
½ tsp	sherry vinegar	2 mL

1. In a stainless steel or other heatproof bowl, combine anchovies, oil, mustard, garlic, honey and vinegar and heat over simmering water in a double boiler, stirring often, until anchovies are dissolved, about 20 minutes. Serve immediately or cover and refrigerate for up to 3 days. If refrigerated, reheat before serving.

Smoked Salmon Mousse

Serve this on thinly sliced baguette, plain biscuits or cocktail-size slices of dark rye bread. It's also delicious spread on Buckwheat Blini (page 178).

Makes about 2 cups (500 mL)

Tip

You may need more cream if using wild salmon, which is likely to have a heavier texture than the farmed variety.

• **Food processor**

8 oz	smoked salmon	250 g
½ to ¾ cup	heavy or whipping (35%) cream (see Tip, left)	125 to 175 mL
1 tbsp	freshly squeezed lemon juice	15 mL
2 tbsp	red lumpfish roe	30 mL
	Freshly ground black pepper	

1. In food processor fitted with metal blade, process smoked salmon, cream and lemon juice until smooth, about 30 seconds. Fold in lumpfish roe. Season liberally with pepper. Spoon into a serving bowl. Serve immediately or cover and refrigerate for up to 2 hours.

Dill-Spiked Crab Scoop

Fresh, light and easy to make, this tasty starter is very festive because crab is a luxury item. Serve it with vegetable sticks, leaves of Belgian endive, baguette or crackers. You can also use it to fill avocado halves (see Variation, below).

Makes about 3 cups (750 mL)		

Tips

If you are using celery hearts, which produce the best results, add any leaves to the work bowl along with the celery.

Our preference is the pasteurized crabmeat, which you can find in cans in the refrigerated section of supermarkets. But regular canned or thawed drained frozen crabmeat works well, too.

• Food processor

½ cup	mayonnaise	125 mL
¼ cup	fresh dill fronds	60 mL
4	green onions, white part with just a hint of green, cut into 3-inch (7.5 cm) chunks	4
1	small shallot, quartered	1
2	stalks celery, cut into 3-inch (7.5 cm) chunks (see Tips, left)	2
2 tbsp	extra virgin olive oil	30 mL
2 tbsp	freshly squeezed lemon juice	30 mL
1 tsp	salt	5 mL
	Freshly ground white pepper	
2 cups	drained cooked crabmeat (about 1 lb/500 g; see Tips, left)	500 mL

1. In food processor fitted with metal blade, pulse mayonnaise, dill, green onions, shallot, celery, olive oil, lemon juice, salt, and white pepper to taste until vegetables are chopped and mixture is blended, about 10 times, stopping and scraping down sides of the bowl as necessary. Add crabmeat and pulse until nicely integrated, about 5 times.

2. Transfer to a serving bowl. Cover and refrigerate for at least 2 hours or overnight.

Variation

Crab-Stuffed Avocado: If you have leftovers, use them to stuff avocado halves. It makes a great lunch or a plated appetizer.

Dill-Spiked Smoked Trout Spread

Save this for special occasions because smoked trout is a bit pricey. On the other hand, it is so easy to make you could serve it any day of the week. It is great on thin wheat crackers (fairly bland so the taste doesn't interfere with the exquisite flavor of the trout) or, if you're feeling celebratory, on Easy Potato Crisps (page 164) or even on Homemade Potato Chips (page 165).

Makes about 2½ cups (625 mL)

Tip

Don't confuse real mayonnaise with "mayonnaise-type" salad dressings, which are similar in appearance. Mayonnaise is a combination of egg yolks, vinegar or lemon juice, olive oil and seasonings. Imitators will contain additional ingredients, such as sugar, flour or milk. Make your own or make sure the label says mayonnaise and check the ingredients.

• Food processor

1 lb	smoked trout fillets, skin and bones removed	500 g
4	green onions, white part with just a bit of green, cut into 3-inch (7.5 cm) lengths	4
1	stalk celery, cut into chunks	1
¼ cup	fresh dill fronds	60 mL
¼ cup	mayonnaise (see Tip, left)	60 mL
2 tbsp	extra virgin olive oil	30 mL
1 tbsp	freshly squeezed lemon juice	15 mL
1 tbsp	Dijon mustard	15 mL

1. In food processor fitted with metal blade, pulse trout, green onions, celery and dill until finely chopped. Add mayonnaise, olive oil, lemon juice and mustard and process until smooth. Transfer to a serving bowl and refrigerate for at least 3 hours or for up to 2 days.

Variation

Trout Stuffed Tomatoes: Cut the tops of cherry tomatoes and using a small spoon, remove some of the pulp. Spoon about 1 tsp (5 mL) of the trout mixture into each tomato.

Sizzling Shrimp and Dill Pickle Dip

This is a great all-season dip, which works well with both light and regular cream cheese and mayonnaise. Serve with celery or carrot sticks, spears of Belgian endives, crackers, biscuits, melba toast or potato chips. Refrigerate any leftovers for future snacks. It keeps well and reheats nicely in the microwave.

Makes 6 servings

Tip

If you prefer, substitute 2 cans (each approx. 3¾ oz/106 g) shrimp, drained.

- **Small (maximum 3½ quart) slow cooker**

8 oz	cream cheese, softened	250 g
¼ cup	mayonnaise	60 mL
1 tbsp	Dijon mustard	15 mL
½ cup	cooked salad shrimp (see Tip, left)	125 mL
¼ cup	finely chopped dill pickle	60 mL
2 tbsp	finely chopped green onion	30 mL
2 tbsp	chopped fresh dill	30 mL

1. In slow cooker stoneware, combine cream cheese, mayonnaise and mustard. Cover and cook on Low for 2 hours or on High for 1 hour.

2. Add shrimp, dill pickle, green onion and dill and stir well to combine. Cover and cook on Low for 1 hour or on High for 30 minutes, until bubbly.

Taramasalata

This delicious concoction is a fixture of Greek mezes. Serve with Crisp Pita Bread (page 172).

Tips

Tarama (carp roe) is available in stores specializing in Greek provisions.

After soaking and squeezing the bread dry, you should have about ½ cup (125 mL).

If you have trouble digesting gluten, substitute your favorite gluten-free bread.

• **Food processor**

½ cup	tarama, thoroughly rinsed under cold running water and drained (see Tips, left)	125 mL
1	small red onion, quartered	1
2	thick slices day-old white bread, crusts removed, soaked in water and squeezed dry (see Tips, left)	2
¼ cup	freshly squeezed lemon juice	60 mL
½ cup	extra virgin olive oil	125 mL
	Pita bread (see Tips, left)	
	Crudités, optional	

1. In food processor fitted with metal blade, process tarama and red onion for 1 minute. Add bread and process until smooth. Add lemon juice and pulse to blend. With motor running, add oil through feed tube and process until pale pink and very creamy.

2. Transfer to a serving bowl. Cover and refrigerate for at least 2 hours or for up to 2 days. Serve with pita bread or crudités, if desired.

Tonnato

Don't be fooled by the simplicity of this recipe: it is a mouthwatering combination. Amazingly versatile, this ambrosial mixture excels as a dip. Make it the centerpiece of a tasting platter, surrounded by celery sticks and cucumber slices or tender leaves of Belgian endive. It also performs well as a topping for asparagus (see Variations, below) or as sauce for plated appetizers.

Makes about 1½ cups (375 mL)

Tips

Don't confuse real mayonnaise with "mayonnaise-type" salad dressings, which are similar in appearance. Mayonnaise is a combination of egg yolks, vinegar or lemon juice, olive oil and seasonings. Imitators will contain additional ingredients, such as sugar, flour or milk. Make your own or make sure the label says mayonnaise and check the ingredients.

To hard-cook eggs: Place eggs in a saucepan in a single layer and add cold water to cover by 1 inch (2.5 cm). Cover and bring to a boil over high heat. Remove from heat and let stand for 10 minutes. Using a slotted spoon, transfer to a bowl of ice water. Let cool for 5 minutes. Remove eggshells under cool running water.

• Food processor

¾ cup	mayonnaise (see Tips, left)	175 mL
½ cup	Italian flat-leaf parsley leaves	125 mL
2	green onions, white part only, cut into 2-inch (5 cm) lengths	2
1 tbsp	drained capers, optional	15 mL
1	can (6 oz/170 g) tuna, preferably Spanish or Italian, packed in olive oil, drained	1
	Freshly ground black pepper	
	Crudités (see page 175)	

1. In food processor fitted with metal blade, process mayonnaise, parsley, green onions, and capers, if using, until smooth. Add tuna and pepper to taste. Pulse until chopped and blended, about 15 times.

2. Transfer to a small bowl and serve surrounded by crudités for dipping. If not using immediately, cover and refrigerate for up to 3 days.

Variations

Tonnato-Stuffed Eggs: (Serves 6 to 8) Hard-cook 4 eggs (see Tips, left). Let cool and peel. Cut in half lengthwise. Pop out the yolks and mash with ¼ cup (60 mL) Tonnato. Mound the mixture back into the whites. Dust with 1 tsp (5 mL) paprika, if desired.

For a plated appetizer, cut eggs in half, arrange them on a platter and spoon the sauce over top.

Asparagus with Tonnato: (Serves 4) Arrange 1 can or jar (16 oz/330 g approx.) white asparagus, drained, on a small platter or serving plate. Top with ¼ cup (60 mL) Tonnato. Use cooked fresh green asparagus in season, if desired. You can also turn this into a salad by spreading a layer of salad greens over a large platter. Arrange the asparagus over the greens and top with Tonnato.

Tuna Tapenade

Known as Provençal caviar, tapenade is a flavorful mixture of capers, olives and anchovies, among other ingredients. Here, the addition of tuna lightens up the result. Serve this with carrot or celery sticks, sliced cucumber, crackers or Basic Crostini (page 176). It also makes a delicious filling for hard-cooked eggs (see Variation, below).

Makes about ¾ cup (175 mL)

Tip

Italian (or Spanish) tuna packed in olive oil is more moist and flavorful than the paler versions packed in water.

• **Food processor**

1	can (6 oz/170 g) tuna, preferably Italian, packed in olive oil, drained (see Tip, left)	1
4	anchovy fillets	4
2 tbsp	drained capers	30 mL
1 tbsp	freshly squeezed lemon juice	15 mL
1	clove garlic, coarsely chopped	1
10	pitted black olives	10
¼ cup	extra virgin olive oil	60 mL

1. In food processor fitted with metal blade, pulse tuna, anchovies, capers, lemon juice, garlic and olives until ingredients are combined but still chunky, about 10 times. Add olive oil and pulse until blended, about 5 times. Spoon into a bowl, cover tightly and refrigerate for at least 2 hours or for up to 3 days.

Variation

Tuna Tapenade–Stuffed Eggs: Follow the instructions for Tonnato-Stuffed Eggs (Variations, page 77) substituting ¼ cup (60 mL) Tuna Tapenade for the Tonnato.

Smoked Oyster Hummus

This intriguing spread is a variation on traditional Middle Eastern hummus. It always gets rave reviews. Serve with pita bread, Crisp Pita Bread (page 172) or crudités, such as celery sticks, peeled baby carrots or sliced cucumbers.

Makes about 3 cups (750 mL)

Tips

If using canned chickpeas, we prefer to use no-salt-added chickpeas, which are usually available in organic or natural good sections in large grocery shores or fine food shops.

For this quality of chickpeas, use 1 can (14 to 19 oz/398 to 540 mL), drained and rinsed or cook 1 cup (250 mL) dried chickpeas.

Use a bottled roasted red pepper or roast your own (see Tips, page 70).

- **Food processor**

2 cups	cooked chickpeas, drained and rinsed (see Tips, left)	500 mL
¼ cup	freshly squeezed lemon juice	60 mL
¼ cup	extra virgin olive oil	60 mL
1	large roasted red bell pepper (see Tips, left)	1
4	cloves garlic	4
½ tsp	salt	2 mL
1	can (3 oz/90 g) smoked oysters, drained	1
	Freshly ground black pepper	

1. In food processor fitted with metal blade, process chickpeas, lemon juice, olive oil, roasted pepper, garlic and salt until smooth, about 30 seconds, stopping and scraping down sides of the bowl as necessary.
2. Add oysters and pulse just to chop and combine, about 5 times. Season to taste with pepper.

Nippy Oyster and Bacon Dip

This rich, creamy dip is very versatile. Spoon into a serving bowl and surround with a big platter of vegetables for dipping, such as blanched broccoli, cauliflower or Brussels sprouts, or crispy potato wedges (see Tip, below). If simplicity is the order of the day, open a bag of potato chips. Either way, this dip always earns rave reviews.

Makes about 2 cups (500 mL)

Tip

To make Crispy Potato Wedges: Bake the desired number of baking potatoes in a 400°F (200°C) oven for 1 hour. Set aside to cool. Thirty minutes before serving the dip, cut each potato into 8 wedges. Brush with olive oil, place in 400°F (200°C) oven and roast until crisp and golden.

- **Small (maximum 3½ quart) slow cooker**

2	slices bacon, cooked to crisp, then crumbled	2
8 oz	cream cheese, softened	250 g
1 cup	shredded Cheddar cheese, preferably sharp (aged)	250 mL
2 tbsp	mayonnaise	30 mL
¼ tsp	freshly ground black pepper	1 mL
½ to 1	jalapeño pepper, seeded and finely chopped	½ to 1
1	can (4 oz/85 g) smoked oysters, drained and cut in half	1
1	roasted red bell pepper, finely chopped (see Tips, page 70)	1
	Potato chips, optional	
	Crispy Potato Wedges (see Tip, left), optional	
	Brussels sprouts, cooked until slightly underdone, optional	
	Blanched broccoli spears or cauliflower florets, optional	

1. In slow cooker stoneware, combine bacon, cream cheese, Cheddar, mayonnaise, black pepper and jalapeño pepper. Stir well. Cover and cook on High for 1 hour. Add oysters and bell pepper and stir again. Cook on High for an additional 30 minutes, until hot and bubbly. Serve immediately with desired vegetables or set temperature to Low until ready to serve.

Variation

Nippy Clam and Bacon Dip: Substitute 1 can (5 oz/142 g) drained clams for the smoked oysters. Add along with the bacon.

BTs on Lettuce

Served on leaves of crisp, cold lettuce, this dip captures the lusciousness of a BLT sandwich made with fresh ripe tomatoes.

- -

Makes about 1½ cups (375 mL)

Tips

We always use flat-leaf rather than curly parsley because it has more flavor.

Chilled wedges of iceberg lettuce, hearts of romaine or even radicchio make a perfect base for this dip.

● **Food processor**

4 oz	cream cheese, softened	125 g
¼ cup	buttermilk	60 mL
2 tbsp	mayonnaise	30 mL
1	clove garlic	1
1	large tomato, peeled, seeded and quartered	1
6	slices bacon, cooked and crumbled	6
½ cup	Italian flat-leaf parsley leaves (see Tips, left)	125 mL
3	green onions, white part with a bit of green, cut into chunks	3
	Lettuce (see Tips, left)	

1. In food processor fitted with metal blade, purée cream cheese, buttermilk, mayonnaise and garlic. Add tomato, bacon, parsley and green onions and pulse until chopped and blended, about 6 times.

2. Transfer to a serving bowl. Serve immediately with crisp cold lettuce or cover and refrigerate for up to 2 days.

Bubbling Bacon and Horseradish Dip

There's nothing like a good dollop of horseradish to add zest to a dish. On a cold winter's day, a bubbling pot of this savory blend is very inviting. Open a big bag of potato chips and have some ready for après-ski or, for a more elegant presentation, serve with Roasted Potato Wedges (page 163), Crisp Potato Wedges (page 27) or on crisp spears of Belgian endive.

Makes 6 servings

Tip

If you want to avoid stirring the dip after an hour, place all the ingredients in a food processor and pulse two or three times until well blended. Transfer to slow cooker stoneware and cook on High as directed.

- **Small (maximum 3½ quart) slow cooker**

2	slices bacon, finely chopped	2
8 oz	cream cheese, softened	250 g
¼ cup	sour cream	60 mL
2 tbsp	mayonnaise	30 mL
2 tbsp	prepared horseradish	30 mL
2 tbsp	finely chopped green onion	30 mL
1	clove garlic, minced	1
¾ cup	shredded Cheddar cheese, preferably sharp (aged)	175 mL
¼ tsp	freshly ground black pepper	1 mL

1. In a skillet over medium-high heat, cook bacon until crisp. Remove with a slotted spoon and drain thoroughly on paper towel.

2. In slow cooker stoneware, combine bacon, cream cheese, sour cream, mayonnaise, horseradish, green onion, garlic, cheese and pepper. Stir well. Cover and cook on High for 1 hour. Stir again and cook on High for an additional 30 minutes, until hot and bubbly. Serve immediately or set temperature at Low until ready to serve. Serve with potato chips or Belgian endive, if desired.

Ham and Roasted Pepper Spread with Hearts of Palm

This spread, which has retro overtones, is updated with the addition of hearts of palm for dipping. This tropical vegetable is widely available in cans and adds an exotic touch to this simple, yet very tasty spread.

Makes
1½ cups (375 mL)

Tips

Use bottled roasted peppers or roast them yourself (see Tips, page 70.)

If you have trouble digesting gluten, check the label to make sure your brand of Worcestershire sauce is gluten-free.

Soaking the hearts of palm in acidulated water (Step 2) removes any tinny taste that may come from the can.

- **Food processor**

2	roasted red bell peppers, coarsely chopped (see Tips, left) or store-bought	2
4 oz	Black Forest ham, coarsely chopped	125 g
1	long green or jalapeño pepper, seeded and quartered	1
3 tbsp	mayonnaise	45 mL
3 tbsp	freshly squeezed lemon juice, divided	45 mL
1 tbsp	extra virgin olive oil	15 mL
½ tsp	Worcestershire sauce (see Tips, left)	2 mL
	Salt and freshly ground black pepper	
2	cans (each 14 oz/398 mL) hearts of palm (see Tips, left)	2

1. In food processor fitted with metal blade, process roasted peppers, ham, chile pepper, mayonnaise, 1 tbsp (15 mL) of the lemon juice, olive oil, Worcestershire sauce, and salt and pepper to taste until smooth. Transfer to a serving bowl. Cover and refrigerate for at least 3 hours or overnight.

2. One hour before you're ready to serve, drain hearts of palm. Place in a long shallow baking dish and add water to cover. Add remaining 2 tbsp (30 mL) of lemon juice. Cover and refrigerate.

3. When you're ready to serve, drain and cut individual hearts lengthwise into halves or quarters, depending upon their size. Place bowl of spread in the center of a platter and surround with palm slices. To serve, spread ham mixture evenly over sliced hearts of palm.

Variation

Instead of hearts of palm serve this spread with celery sticks, cucumber slices or pita bread.

Savory Salsas

Fresh Tomato Salsa

This is a Mexican fresh salsa, often called pico de gallo. Make it when tomatoes are in season — otherwise the results are likely to be disappointing. It's delicious with tortilla chips. It also makes a great accompaniment to Fresh Corn Cakes (page 166) and Cheese and Corn Arepas (pages 179 and 180).

Makes about 2¼ cups (550 mL)

Tips

Using puréed rather than minced garlic ensures it is evenly distributed throughout the salsa, producing just a welcome hint of flavor.

To purée garlic: Use a fine sharp-toothed grater such as those made by Microplane.

We recommend using pure sea salt rather than refined table salt. It has a clean, crisp taste and enhanced mineral content, unlike table salt, which has a bitter acrid taste and contains unpleasant additives to prevent caking.

2 cups	diced (¼ inch/0.5 cm) ripe field tomatoes	500 mL
¼ cup	very finely chopped red or green onion	60 mL
¼ cup	very finely chopped fresh cilantro leaves	60 mL
1 to 2	jalapeño peppers or 2 to 4 serrano chiles, seeded and minced	1 to 2
1	clove garlic, puréed (see Tips, left)	1
1 tbsp	freshly squeezed lime juice	15 mL
½ to 1 tsp	salt	2 to 5 mL

1. In a bowl, combine tomatoes, green onion, cilantro, chile pepper to taste, garlic, lime juice and salt to taste. Toss to combine. Set aside at room temperature for 15 minutes to meld flavors. Serve within 3 hours of preparation. Left to sit the tomatoes become soggy and the onion and garlic start to dominate.

Summer Tomato Salsa

Nothing says summer like a beautiful tomato. Basic Crostini (page 176), Pita Chips (see Variations, page 173) or tortilla chips would be the usual pairings and all are fantastic. For something a little different, try Fresh Corn Cakes (page 166).

Makes about 1½ cups (375 mL)

Tip

Chiffonade is a French culinary term for slicing into thin ribbons. In this case it is basil. Stack washed and dried leaves of basil into a neat pile and roll into a small cigar shape. With a sharp knife, slice across the cigar to form thin ribbons and delicately fluff the basil with your hands to separate.

1¼ cups	diced tomato	300 mL
½ cup	finely diced shallots	125 mL
5 tsp	extra virgin olive oil	25 mL
1 tbsp	chiffonade fresh basil (see Tip, left)	15 mL
1 tsp	balsamic vinegar	5 mL
½ tsp	salt	2 mL
⅛ tsp	freshly ground black pepper	0.5 mL

1. In a bowl, combine tomato, shallots, olive oil, basil, vinegar, salt and pepper. Cover and let stand at room temperature for at least 1 hour to allow flavors to meld or for up to 4 hours.

Green Tomato Salsa

Vegan Friendly

This recipe proves that green tomatoes can be as tasty as those pretty red ones. Crunchy tortilla chips, crisp Beet Chips (page 169) or Crisp Pita Bread (page 172) would all pair perfectly with this flavorful salsa.

Makes about 1½ cups (375 mL)

Tip

For best flavor, toast and grind cumin yourself.
To toast seeds: Place seeds in a dry skillet over medium heat and cook, stirring, until fragrant, about 3 minutes. Immediately transfer to a mortar or spice grinder and grind.

1¼ cups	diced green tomatoes	300 mL
¼ cup	finely diced onion	60 mL
¼ cup	diced red tomato	60 mL
2 tbsp	freshly squeezed lime juice	30 mL
1 tsp	minced garlic	5 mL
½ tsp	ground cumin (see Tip, left)	2 mL
¼ tsp	finely diced seeded jalapeño	1 mL
¼ tsp	salt	1 mL

1. In a bowl, combine green tomatoes, onion, red tomato, lime juice, garlic, cumin, jalapeño and salt. Cover and let stand at room temperature for 1 hour to allow flavors to meld or for up to 4 hours.

Fresh Salsa Verde

This is a Mexican "raw" salsa made with lightly cooked tomatillos instead of tomatoes. Although you can use drained canned tomatillos, the taste is much brighter when made with those that are fresh. Increasingly, this bitter fruit is being grown throughout North America, so look for it at farmers' markets. Serve with tortilla chips, or Cheese or Corn Arepas (pages 179 and 180).

Makes about 1 cup (250 mL)

Tips

If you're buying fresh tomatillos, this is the quantity in a pint (500 mL) basket.

If you prefer, substitute 2 to 4 Mexican serrano chiles for the jalapeños.

If you are a heat seeker, use a second jalapeño. One makes a pleasantly mild salsa.

- **Food processor**

2 cups	fresh tomatillos (about 9), husked (see Tips, left)	500 mL
1 to 2	jalapeño peppers, coarsely chopped (see Tips, left)	1 to 2
2 tbsp	coarsely chopped red or green onion	30 mL
1	clove garlic, coarsely chopped	1
½ cup	packed fresh cilantro leaves	125 mL
½ tsp	salt	2 mL

1. In a small saucepan over medium heat, combine tomatillos and water to cover. Bring to a boil. Reduce heat and simmer just until tender, about 10 minutes. Drain, let cool slightly and transfer to a food processor fitted with metal blade. Pulse to chop, 2 or 3 times. Add jalapeños to taste, onion, garlic, cilantro and salt and pulse until jalapeños are finely chopped and mixture is well integrated, about 10 times. Set aside at room temperature for 15 minutes to allow flavors to meld. Serve within 3 hours of preparation.

Bloody Mary Salsa

Vegan Friendly

Here's a wonderful alternative to the real deal! For the perfect pairing serve this atop peeled celery stalks or even as a garnish for fresh shucked oysters.

Makes about 1½ cups (375 mL)

Tips

Cornichons are the French version of gherkins and may be used here.

Celery tends to be very fibrous and "stringy." Using a vegetable peeler, peel the celery, exposing the white, delicate flesh.

1⅔ cups	diced tomato	400 mL
1 tbsp	finely diced seeded jalapeño	15 mL
1 tbsp	finely diced gherkins (see Tips, left)	15 mL
1 tbsp	vodka	15 mL
1 tsp	vegan or regular Worcestershire sauce	5 mL
1 tsp	finely diced celery (see Tips, left)	5 mL
½ tsp	hot pepper sauce	2 mL
½ tsp	salt	2 mL

1. In a bowl, combine tomato, jalapeño, gherkins, vodka, Worcestershire sauce, celery, hot pepper sauce and salt. Refrigerate and marinate for 1 hour or for up to 4 hours.

Tomato Balsamic "Jam"

If you're looking for a twist on the regular tomato salsa, this is definitely it! This is a fantastic accompaniment to Basic Crostini (page 176) or sliced cucumber or atop halved cherry tomatoes.

Makes about 1 cup (250 mL)

Tip

We recommend using pure sea salt rather than refined table salt. It has a clean, crisp taste and enhanced mineral content, unlike table salt, which has a bitter acrid taste and contains unpleasant additives to prevent caking.

2 tbsp	balsamic vinegar	30 mL
1½ cups	diced seeded tomato	375 mL
1 tsp	coarsely chopped fresh oregano leaves	5 mL
¼ tsp	salt	1 mL
	Freshly ground black pepper	

1. In a small saucepan, bring balsamic vinegar to a boil over medium-high heat. Reduce heat and simmer until vinegar is reduced to a syrup consistency, about 3 minutes. Remove from heat and add tomatoes, oregano, salt, and pepper to taste. Let cool to room temperature and serve.

Tomato and Spinach Salsa

This tasty salsa can garnish the perfect Basic Crostini (page 176) or Homemade Potato Chips (page 165).

Makes about 1½ cups (375 mL)

Tip

Chiffonade is a French culinary term for slicing into thin ribbons — in this case spinach. Stack spinach leaves into a neat pile and roll into a small cigar shape. With a sharp knife, slice across the cigar to form thin ribbons and delicately fluff the spinach with your hands to separate.

1¼ cups	diced ripe tomato	300 mL
1 cup	chiffonade spinach leaves (see Tip, left)	250 mL
2 tbsp	extra virgin olive oil	30 mL
1 tsp	freshly squeezed lemon juice	5 mL
1	clove garlic, thinly sliced or minced	1
¼ tsp	chopped fresh thyme leaves	1 mL
⅛ tsp	salt	0.5 mL
⅛ tsp	freshly ground black pepper	0.5 mL

1. In a bowl, combine tomato, spinach, olive oil, lemon juice, garlic, thyme, salt and pepper. Serve within 3 hours of preparation.

Roasted Onion Salsa

It is amazing what happens to an onion when roasted — it becomes as sweet as sugar. This sweetness contrasts wonderfully with hot dogs. The salsa is perfect with salty tortilla chips or Bagel Chips (page 177), as well as with good potato chips.

Makes about 1¼ cups (300 mL)

Tip

The sweetness of Roasted Onion Salsa pairs beautifully with soft, creamy cheeses such as Camembert or Brie de Meaux. Topped on Bagel Chips (page 177) or Crisp Pita Bread (page 172), this would make a great first impression on your dinner guests.

• **Preheat oven to 400°F (200°C)**

2	onions (unpeeled)	2
¼ cup	finely diced red bell pepper	60 mL
1 tbsp	red wine vinegar	15 mL
½ tsp	Dijon mustard	2 mL
¼ tsp	chopped fresh thyme leaves	1 mL
¼ tsp	chopped fresh oregano leaves	1 mL

1. Place onions on a baking sheet and roast in preheated oven until skins are browned and crisp and onions are fork tender, about 1 hour. Transfer to a bowl and let stand until cool enough to handle, preferably overnight, covered and refrigerated. Peel off skins and dice onions, reserving any accumulated juices.

2. In a bowl, combine roasted onions and any reserved liquid, bell pepper, vinegar, Dijon, thyme and oregano. Cover and refrigerate for at least 1 hour to allow flavors to meld or for up to 3 days before serving.

Roasted Beet Salsa

Beets are like candy after roasting. Serve with crisp Beet Chips (page 169), Taro Root Chips (page 170) or Bagel Chips (page 177).

Makes about 1 1/4 cups (300 mL)

Tip

Slivered almonds are very thin and can burn quite quickly if not watched closely. Because of this, we prefer to toast them on the stovetop. *To toast almonds:* In a skillet over medium-high heat add enough almonds just to cover the bottom of the skillet and, stirring constantly, toast until fragrant and golden brown, 2 to 3 minutes.

• Preheat oven to 200°F (100°C)

1 1/2 lbs	beets, unpeeled	750 g
	Olive oil	
	Salt	
1/4 cup	toasted slivered almonds (see Tip, left)	60 mL
1 tbsp	sherry vinegar	15 mL
1 tbsp	extra virgin olive oil	15 mL
1/2 tsp	fresh thyme leaves	2 mL

1. Place beets on a rimmed baking sheet or in a baking dish. Toss with oil, sprinkle with 1 tsp (5 mL) salt and cover with foil. Roast in preheated oven until tender, about 2 hours. Remove from oven, spoon off 2 tbsp (30 mL) of the cooking juice and set aside. Discard any excess juice. Let beets cool just until they are cool enough to touch, then using a piece of paper towel, rub off skins and dice.

2. In a bowl, combine 1 1/4 cups (300 mL) diced beets, almonds, vinegar, olive oil, thyme and 1/8 tsp (0.5 mL) salt. Cover and refrigerate for at least 1 hour to allow flavors to meld or for up to 3 days before serving.

Eggplant and Date Salsa

This salsa is a Middle Eastern flavor explosion. It's just amazing as a topping for Hummus from Scratch (page 137) spread over warm wedges of pita or Pita Chips (see Variations, page 173).

2 tbsp	olive oil	30 mL
2 cups	diced unpeeled eggplant	500 mL
¾ tsp	salt	3 mL
¼ tsp	chopped fresh thyme leaves	1 mL
½ cup	finely diced tomato	125 mL
¼ cup	finely diced dried dates	60 mL
¼ cup	finely diced sweet onion	60 mL
1 tbsp	sweet barbecue sauce (see Tips, left)	15 mL
1 tsp	minced black olives (see Tips, left)	5 mL
1 tsp	freshly squeezed lemon juice	5 mL
¼ tsp	cracked black peppercorns	1 mL

Makes about 1½ cups (375 mL)

Tips

If you have trouble digesting gluten, check the label to make sure your barbecue sauce is gluten-free.

We prefer the pungent taste of Greek kalamata olives but almost any black olive would work well here. Just be sure not to use those that come in cans because they have no flavor.

1. In a large skillet, heat oil over medium heat. Add eggplant, salt and thyme and cook, stirring, until eggplant is soft, about 10 minutes. Transfer to a bowl and let cool to room temperature.

2. Add tomato, dates, onion, barbecue sauce, olives, lemon juice and peppercorns to eggplant mixture and mix well. Cover and let stand at room temperature for at least 1 hour to allow flavors to meld or refrigerate for up to 1 day before serving.

Variation

Dates are quite easy to find in grocery stores but in this recipe could easily be replaced by prunes, dried apricots or dried peaches.

Warm Eggplant Salsa

This is a great accompaniment to Hummus from Scratch (page 137). Serve with pita bread, Bagel Chips (page 177) or even crisp Beet Chips (page 169).

Makes about 1½ cups (375 mL)

Tip

Chiffonade is a French culinary term for slicing into thin ribbons. In this case it is basil. Stack washed and dried leaves of basil into a neat pile and roll into a small cigar shape. With a sharp knife, slice across the cigar to form thin ribbons and delicately fluff the basil with your hands to separate.

2 tbsp	olive oil	30 mL
2 cups	diced unpeeled eggplant	500 mL
¾ tsp	salt	3 mL
½ cup	finely diced roasted red bell pepper (see Tip, page 98)	125 mL
½ cup	finely diced tomato	125 mL
¼ cup	finely diced shallot	60 mL
2 tbsp	sherry vinegar	30 mL
¼ tsp	cracked black peppercorns	1 mL
1	basil leaf, chiffonade (see Tip, left)	1

1. In a large skillet, heat oil over medium heat. Add eggplant and salt and cook, stirring, until eggplant is soft, about 10 minutes. Transfer to a bowl and let cool to room temperature.

2. Add roasted pepper, tomato, shallot, vinegar, peppercorns and basil to eggplant and mix well. Serve immediately. If you prefer, you can serve this cold, in which case after completing Step 2, cover and refrigerate for up to 1 day.

Jicama Salsa

Jicama is a crunchy refreshing vegetable that resembles a cross between an apple and potato. The combination of jicama with citrus creates a tropical island experience. This salsa can be served with something as simple as a slice of cheese.

Makes about 1½ cups (375 mL)

Tip

Agave syrup is produced from the agave plant and because it contains a high percentage of fructose, it is much sweeter than honey.

1½ cups	diced peeled jicama	375 mL
1 tsp	grated orange zest	5 mL
⅓ cup	freshly squeezed orange juice	75 mL
¼ cup	orange segments	60 mL
1 tsp	minced chives	5 mL
1 tsp	finely chopped fresh basil leaves	5 mL
1 tsp	finely chopped fresh mint leaves	5 mL
½ tsp	agave syrup (see Tip, left)	2 mL
⅛ tsp	salt	0.5 mL
⅛ tsp	freshly ground black pepper	0.5 mL

1. In a bowl, combine jicama, orange zest and juice, orange segments, chives, basil, mint, agave syrup, salt and pepper. Refrigerate and marinate for at least 1 hour or for up to 3 days before serving.

Roasted Red Pepper Salsa

Try this incredibly sweet-and-smoky flavored salsa; it might just replace tomato salsa. Try it with tortilla chips, wedges of red bell pepper, or for something a little more extravagant, on top of appetizer-size wedges of a grilled cheese sandwich.

Makes about 1¼ cups (300 mL)

Tip

To roast peppers: Preheat broiler. Place pepper(s) on a baking sheet and broil, turning two or three times, until skin on all sides is blackened, about 25 minutes. Transfer to a heatproof bowl. Cover with a plate and let stand until cool. Remove and, using a sharp knife, lift skins off. Discard skins, core and seeds.

¾ cup	diced roasted red bell pepper (see Tip, left)	175 mL
½ cup	diced tomato	125 mL
¼ cup	finely diced red onion	60 mL
1 tbsp	red wine vinegar	15 mL
1 tbsp	agave syrup	15 mL
1 tsp	minced rinsed capers	5 mL

1. In a bowl, combine roasted pepper, tomato, red onion, vinegar, agave syrup and capers. Serve immediately or cover and let stand at room temperature for up to 4 hours.

Red Radish and Goat Cheese Salsa

The delicate peppery flavor combined with a tart creamy goat cheese is perfect with freshly cut Belgian endive spear or Basic Crostini (page 176).

Makes about 1½ cups (375 mL)

Tip

Red radishes are usually available in your local grocery store. As an alternative, the equally sharp-flavored Daikon radish or even white turnip would work well in this recipe.

1 cup	diced red radishes (see Tip, left)	250 mL
¼ cup	finely diced white onion	60 mL
1 tbsp	soft goat cheese	15 mL
1 tbsp	coarsely chopped fresh basil leaves	15 mL
2 tsp	Champagne vinegar or white wine	10 mL

1. In a bowl, combine red radishes, onion, goat cheese, basil and vinegar. Cover and refrigerate for at least 1 hour to allow flavors to meld or for up to 3 days before serving.

Asparagus Salsa

Vegan Friendly

Serve this one-of-a-kind food experience on top of Basic Crostini (page 176).

Makes about 1½ cups (375 mL)

Tips

When blanching green vegetables, salt is very useful for adding flavor. It is also quite instrumental in bringing the vibrant green color out long before the vegetable is overcooked. For maximum effect, we suggest 1 tbsp (15 mL) salt for every 6 cups (1.5 L) of water.

We recommend using pure sea salt rather than refined table salt. It has a clean, crisp taste and enhanced mineral content, unlike table salt, which has a bitter acrid taste and contains unpleasant additives to prevent caking.

1¼ cups	finely chopped asparagus	300 mL
	Ice water	
⅓ cup	finely diced cherry tomatoes	75 mL
⅓ cup	grilled corn kernels (see Tip, page 104)	75 mL
2 tbsp	finely diced red onion	30 mL
1 tbsp	coarsely chopped dried cranberries	15 mL
1 tbsp	coarsely chopped toasted almonds	15 mL
1 tsp	malt vinegar	5 mL
1 tsp	extra virgin olive oil	5 mL
½ tsp	chopped fresh basil leaves	2 mL
¼ tsp	salt	1 mL
¼ tsp	freshly ground black pepper	1 mL
⅛ tsp	hot pepper flakes	0.5 mL

1. In a pot of boiling salted water, blanch asparagus until vibrant green and al dente, about 2 minutes. Drain and immediately plunge into a bowl of ice water to stop the cooking process. Let stand until well chilled. Drain well.

2. In a bowl, combine asparagus, tomatoes, corn, red onion, cranberries, almonds, vinegar, olive oil, basil, salt, pepper and hot pepper flakes. Let stand at room temperature for at least 1 hour to allow flavors to meld or cover and refrigerate for up to 8 hours before serving.

Green Bean Salsa

A very fresh salsa that is wonderful in the summer time atop thick slices of plum tomatoes, sliced English cucumbers or hearts of romaine leaves.

Makes about 1²⁄₃ cups (400 mL)

Tip

Haricots vert or French beans would work very nicely in this recipe.

1⅓ cups	finely chopped green beans (see Tip, left)	325 mL
	Ice water	
¼ cup	diced tomato	60 mL
1 tsp	thinly sliced or minced garlic	5 mL
1 tsp	basil pesto	5 mL
¼ tsp	salt	1 mL

1. In a pot of boiling salted water, blanch green beans until bright green and al dente, 4 to 5 minutes. Drain and immediately plunge into a bowl of ice water to stop the cooking. Let stand until well chilled. Drain well.

2. In a bowl, combine green beans, tomato, garlic, basil pesto and salt. Serve immediately or cover and refrigerate for up to 8 hours.

Portobello Mushroom and Feta Cheese Salsa

A very simple and hearty salsa that is quite versatile. Use atop a grilled pizza or Yogurt Flatbread (page 174) or just plunge Pita Chips (see Variations, page 173) or Bagel Chips (page 177) into the salsa for a real explosion of textures and flavor.

Makes about 2 cups (500 mL)

Tip

Chiffonade is a French culinary term for slicing into thin ribbons. In this case it is basil. Stack washed and dried leaves of basil into a neat pile and roll into a small cigar shape. With a sharp knife, slice across the cigar to form thin ribbons and delicately fluff the basil with your hands to separate.

• **Preheat barbecue grill to high**

4	portobello mushrooms	4
2 tbsp	olive oil	30 mL
1 tbsp	balsamic vinegar	15 mL
1/4 cup	feta cheese	60 mL
2 tbsp	thinly sliced green onions, green part only	30 mL
1 tbsp	minced drained oil-packed sun-dried tomato	15 mL
1 tbsp	chiffonade fresh basil leaves (see Tip, left)	15 mL
1 tsp	sherry vinegar	5 mL
1/2 tsp	salt	2 mL

1. Remove stems from mushrooms and peel outside layer off caps. In a shallow dish, combine oil and balsamic vinegar. Add mushroom caps and turn to coat. Place stem side up on preheated grill, close lid and grill until liquid begins to form in the cavity where the stem used to be, 5 to 6 minutes. Flip over and grill until tender, about 3 minutes. Transfer to a bowl and let cool.

2. Dice mushrooms, reserving any accumulated liquid in bowl. Return chopped mushrooms to bowl and add feta cheese, green onions, sun-dried tomato, basil, vinegar and salt and mix well. Serve immediately or cover and refrigerate for up to 3 days.

Warm Mushroom Salsa

Here's a simple appetizer created for those sudden pop-in guests — the only problem? They may just "pop in" more often. Pair with Homemade Potato Chips (page 165) or Basic Crostini (page 176).

Makes about 1½ cups (375 mL)

Tip

Stack washed and dried Brussels sprout leaves into a neat pile and lay flat on a cutting board. With a sharp knife, slice across the leaves to create thin ribbons, also known as chiffonade.

2 tbsp	extra virgin olive oil	30 mL
4 cups	quartered mushrooms	1 L
2	cloves garlic, thinly sliced	2
¾ cup	thinly sliced or chiffonade Brussels sprouts leaves (see Tip, left)	175 mL
1 tsp	chopped fresh thyme leaves	5 mL
½ tsp	salt	2 mL
¼ tsp	freshly ground black pepper	1 mL
1 tbsp	sherry vinegar	15 mL

1. In a large skillet, heat oil over medium heat. Add mushrooms and cook, stirring, until soft, 7 to 8 minutes. Add garlic, Brussels sprouts, thyme, salt and pepper and cook, stirring, until Brussels sprout leaves are tender, about 5 minutes. Remove from heat and add vinegar. Transfer to a bowl and serve immediately or cover and refrigerate for up to 3 days. To reheat, warm on low heat, stirring often until warmed through, 3 to 5 minutes.

Roasted Corn Salsa

This is one of the sweetest salsas you will ever taste. Pita Chips (see Variations, page 173) or Fresh Corn Cakes (page 166) or Cheese or Corn Arepas (pages 179 and 180) would all be wonderful accompaniments.

Makes about 1⅔ cups (400 mL)

Tip

To grill corn: Preheat barbecue grill to High. Grill ears of corn, husks on, rotating often until dark brown all over, about 20 minutes. Transfer to a plate and let cool for 5 minutes or until cool enough to handle. Remove husk and silks and using a serrated knife, cut kernels from cob.

1 cup	grilled corn kernels (see Tip, left)	250 mL
½ cup	diced tomato	125 mL
2 tbsp	thinly sliced green onions	30 mL
2 tbsp	finely diced red onion	30 mL
2 tbsp	coarsely chopped fresh cilantro leaves	30 mL
2 tsp	freshly squeezed lemon juice	10 mL
¼ tsp	salt	1 mL

1. In a bowl, combine corn, tomato, green onions, red onion, cilantro, lemon juice and salt. Let stand at room temperature for at least 1 hour to allow flavors to meld or cover and refrigerate for up to 1 day before serving.

Cucumber and Roasted Corn Salsa

Here's a refreshing salsa that is so perfectly filled with summer flavors you can serve it all on its own on a Chinese soup spoon. Serve with slices of English cucumbers or crunchy Beet Chips (page 169) to add one more textural dimension. Either way, it is superb.

Makes about 1½ cups (375 mL)

Tip

We recommend using pure sea salt rather than refined table salt. It has a clean, crisp taste and enhanced mineral content, unlike table salt, which has a bitter acrid taste and contains unpleasant additives to prevent caking.

1 cup	finely diced peeled seeded English cucumber	250 mL
½ cup	grilled corn kernels (see Tip, page 104)	125 mL
1 tbsp	sliced cherry tomatoes	15 mL
1 tbsp	apple cider vinegar	15 mL
1 tbsp	mayonnaise	15 mL
1 tsp	agave syrup or liquid honey	5 mL
1 tsp	coarsely chopped fresh basil	5 mL
¼ tsp	salt	1 mL
	Freshly ground black pepper	

1. In a bowl, combine cucumber, corn, tomatoes, vinegar, mayonnaise, agave syrup, basil, salt, and pepper to taste. Cover and refrigerate for at least 1 hour to allow flavors to meld or for up to 1 day before serving.

Avocado Corn Salsa

Vegan Friendly

Refreshing and delicious, this savory salsa is perfect with crisp tostadas or tortilla chips. If you're feeling festive, launch the evening with a round of margaritas.

	Makes about 4 cups (1 L)	

Tip

If you have cold-pressed avocado oil, by all means substitute it for the olive oil.

1½ cups	cooked corn kernels, cooled	375 mL
1 tsp	extra virgin olive oil (see Tip, left)	5 mL
2	avocados, diced	2
½	red bell pepper, diced	½
½ cup	finely diced red onion	125 mL
½	habanero pepper, seeded and diced	½
¼ cup	freshly squeezed lime juice (about 1 lime)	60 mL
¼ cup	freshly squeezed orange juice (about ½ an orange)	60 mL
2 tbsp	minced fresh oregano leaves	30 mL
	Salt and freshly ground black pepper	

1. In a bowl, combine corn and olive oil. Toss well. Add avocados, bell pepper, red onion, habanero, lime juice, orange juice and oregano. Toss well to combine. Season to taste with salt and black pepper. Refrigerate for about 30 minutes to allow flavors to meld.

Guacamole

Guacamole is a classic for a reason. Although in North America we usually make a smooth version in a food processor and treat it like a dip, in Mexico, where it is identified as a salsa, it is made with a *molcajete*, and it's usually quite chunky. It is very easy to make, loaded with nutrition and absolutely delicious. Serve this with tostadas or tortilla chips. Anything else would be superfluous.

Makes
2 cups (500 mL)

Tips

If fresh tomatoes aren't in season, you may want to substitute cherry or grape tomatoes instead. You'll need 10 for this quantity.

If you are a heat seeker, use a second jalapeño. One makes a pleasantly mild guacamole.

• Food processor

3	small avocados, such as Hass	3
1	tomato, cored and peeled (see Tips, left)	1
4	green onions, white part only, or 1 slice (about ½ inch/1 cm) red onion	4
1 to 2	jalapeño peppers, seeded and cut in half (see Tips, left)	1 to 2
½ cup	fresh cilantro leaves	125 mL
3 tbsp	freshly squeezed lime juice	45 mL
	Salt	

1. In food processor fitted with metal blade, process avocados, tomato, green onions, jalapeño pepper to taste, cilantro and lime juice until desired texture is achieved. (We like ours a bit chunky.) Season to taste with salt. Transfer to a serving bowl.

Pepper Confetti Salsa

This very colorful salsa will brighten any crisp chip that it adorns. Try it with Basic Crostini (page 176), sweet Parsnip Chips (page 171) or tortilla chips.

Makes about 1 ½ cups (375 mL)

Tip

We recommend using pure sea salt rather than refined table salt. It has a clean, crisp taste and enhanced mineral content, unlike table salt, which has a bitter acrid taste and contains unpleasant additives to prevent caking.

½ cup	finely diced tomato	125 mL
⅓ cup	each finely diced red, orange and yellow bell peppers	75 mL
⅓ cup	finely diced peeled English cucumber	75 mL
1 tbsp	finely diced red onion	15 mL
1 tbsp	vodka	15 mL
1 tsp	minced garlic	5 mL
1 tsp	extra virgin olive oil	5 mL
½ tsp	grated lemon zest	2 mL
½ tsp	freshly squeezed lemon juice	2 mL
¼ tsp	salt	1 mL
¼ tsp	herbes de Provence	1 mL
¼ tsp	hot pepper sauce	1 mL
¼ tsp	vegan or regular Worcestershire sauce	1 mL

1. In a large bowl, combine tomato, bell peppers, cucumber, onion, vodka, garlic, oil, lemon zest and juice, salt, herbes de Provence, hot sauce and Worcestershire. Serve or cover and let stand for up to 4 hours.

Suneeta's Cilantro Mint Chutney

This recipe is adapted from one that appeared in *Easy Indian Cooking* by Suneeta Vaswani. It makes a very fresh-tasting salsa that is delicious on Green Plantain Chips (page 167) or tortilla chips. It also makes a wonderful dipping sauce for cold boiled shrimp or samosas.

**Makes
1 cup (250 mL)**

Tips

For best flavor, we like to toast and grind cumin ourselves. *To toast seeds:* Place seeds in a dry skillet over medium heat and cook, stirring, until fragrant about 3 minutes. Immediately transfer to a mortar or a spice grinder and grind.

If you are vegan, use unbleached organic sugar to ensure it has not been filtered through bone char.

• **Food processor**

4 cups	loosely packed cilantro leaves	1 L
1	long red chile pepper	1
½ cup	fresh mint leaves	125 mL
¼ cup	freshly squeezed lime juice	60 mL
2 tbsp	minced gingerroot	30 mL
1 tsp	minced garlic	5 mL
1 tsp	ground cumin (see Tips, left)	5 mL
2 tsp	granulated sugar (see Tips, left)	10 mL
½ tsp	salt	2 mL

1. In food processor fitted with a metal blade, process cilantro, chile pepper, mint, lime juice, ginger, garlic, cumin, sugar and salt until smoothly puréed, stopping and scraping down the sides of the bowl as necessary.

Yogurt Mint Chutney

Thanks to Suneeta Vaswani for allowing us to use this recipe, which appeared in her book *Easy Indian Cooking*. It is simple to make and very delicious. It makes a great dipping sauce for samosas or Yogurt Flatbread (page 174).

**Makes
1 cup (250 mL)**

• **Blender**

1 cup	plain yogurt, divided	250 mL
8	mint leaves	8
½ to 1	long green or red chile pepper	½ to 1
2 tbsp	fresh cilantro leaves	30 mL
¼ tsp	salt or to taste	1 mL

1. In a blender, blend ¼ cup (60 mL) of the yogurt, mint, chile pepper, cilantro and salt into a smooth paste. Transfer to a bowl. Stir into remaining yogurt.
2. Cover and refrigerate until chilled before serving. (Chutney can be stored in an airtight container in the refrigerator for up to 1 week. Do not freeze.)

Warm Salami and Red Pepper Salsa

This is absolutely incredible with Basic Crostini (page 176) or flatbread.

**Makes about
1 cup (250 mL)**

Tip

There are numerous types of salami, such as Genoa or saucisson, and all vary in texture, heat and even the type of meat used. For this recipe we suggest using a mild beef salami that has a smooth texture. If you have trouble digesting gluten, check the label to make sure it's gluten-free.

1 cup	diced salami (see Tip, left)	250 mL
⅓ cup	diced red bell pepper	75 mL
1 tbsp	agave syrup	15 mL
1 tbsp	apple cider vinegar	15 mL
1 tbsp	thinly sliced green onion, green part only	15 mL
1 tsp	thinly sliced long red chile pepper	5 mL

1. In a medium saucepan over high heat, sauté salami until warmed through, about 5 minutes. Remove from heat and add bell pepper, agave syrup, vinegar, green onion and chile pepper and stir well to combine. Transfer to a bowl and serve immediately or cover and refrigerate for up to 3 days. Serve warm or bring to room temperature before serving.

Shrimp Salsa

If you're looking for a salsa that is a bit more substantial than one made exclusively with vegetables or fruit, try this. It is great with tortilla chips, Green Plantain Chips (page 167) or even sliced cucumber.

Makes about 2 cups (500 mL)

Tip

To purée garlic: Use a fine, sharp-toothed grater such as Microplane.

8 oz	cooked salad shrimp (about 1½ cups/375 mL)	250 g
1 tbsp	extra virgin olive oil	15 mL
1	clove garlic, puréed (see Tip, left)	1
1	avocado, diced	1
2	tomatoes, peeled and diced (about 1 cup/250 mL)	2
¼ cup	finely diced red onion	60 mL
1	jalapeño pepper, seeded and minced	1
¼ cup	freshly squeezed lime juice	60 mL
1 tsp	salt	5 mL
	Freshly ground black pepper	

1. In a bowl, combine shrimp, olive oil and garlic. Toss well. Add avocado, tomatoes, red onion, jalapeño, lime juice, salt, and black pepper to taste. Mix well. Cover and refrigerate for 1 hour.

Fruit Salsas

Pineapple Banana Salsa

Except for the fresh pineapple, you can make this luscious salsa from ingredients you're likely to have on hand. This is delicious on tortilla chips and tostadas or Green Plantain Chips (page 167).

Makes about 4 cups (1 L)

Tips

If you don't have access to a mild chile pepper such as serrano, substitute about half of a jalapeño pepper instead.

Because you're using the zest of the orange, we recommend using organically grown fruit.

3 cups	diced fresh pineapple (about ½ a small one)	750 mL
3	bananas, peeled and very thinly sliced (about ⅛ inch/3 mm)	3
1	mild chile pepper, such as serrano, seeded and minced (see Tips, left)	1
1 tsp	finely grated orange zest (see Tips, left)	5 mL
⅓ cup	freshly squeezed orange juice	75 mL
2 tbsp	finely chopped mint	30 mL
2 tbsp	finely chopped cashews, optional	30 mL

1. In a bowl, combine pineapple, bananas, chile pepper, orange zest and juice, mint, and cashews, if using. Toss well. Set aside for 10 minutes to meld flavors.

2. Transfer to a serving bowl and serve immediately. Because this salsa contains bananas, it doesn't keep well. It is best served within a few hours of being prepared.

Black Bean and Pineapple Salsa

This Caribbean-inspired salsa pairs perfectly with Green Plantain Chips (page 167) or tortilla chips.

Makes about 2 cups (500 mL)

Tip

For best results toast and grind the coriander seeds yourself. *To toast seeds:* Place seeds in a dry skillet over medium heat and cook, stirring, until fragrant, about 3 minutes. Immediately transfer to a mortar or a spice grinder and grind.

1 cup	cooked drained black beans (see Tips, page 147)	250 mL
½ cup	finely diced pineapple	125 mL
¼ cup	finely diced red bell pepper	60 mL
¼ cup	finely diced lime segments	60 mL
2 tbsp	finely diced red onion	30 mL
2 tbsp	coarsely chopped fresh cilantro leaves	30 mL
½ tsp	finely chopped seeded jalapeño pepper	2 mL
3 tbsp	freshly squeezed lime juice	45 mL
2 tbsp	extra virgin olive oil	30 mL
1 tbsp	agave syrup	15 mL
1 tsp	chipotle powder	5 mL
½ tsp	salt	2 mL
½ tsp	ground coriander (see Tip, left)	2 mL

1. In a bowl, combine black beans, pineapple, bell pepper, lime segments, red onion, cilantro and jalapeño pepper.

2. Add lime juice, olive oil, agave syrup, chipotle powder, salt and coriander and mix well. Serve immediately or cover and refrigerate for up to 1 day.

Chipotle Pineapple Salsa

A sweet and spicy salsa that will not only delight your palate but all of your guests, too. Try this with tortilla chips, Green Plantain Chips (page 167) or crispy Beet Chips (page 169).

Makes about 1¼ cups (300 mL)

Tip

Chipotle powder adds a wonderful smoky complement to the sweet flavor of pineapple. As an alternative, smoked paprika would offer the same smoky profile.

1¼ cups	diced pineapple	300 mL
1 tsp	sherry vinegar	5 mL
½ tsp	minced chives	2 mL
½ tsp	coarsely chopped fresh cilantro leaves	2 mL
¼ tsp	chipotle powder (see Tip, left)	1 mL

1. In a bowl, combine pineapple, vinegar, chives, cilantro and chipotle powder. Cover and refrigerate for at least 1 hour to allow flavors to meld or for up to 1 day before serving.

Minty Mango Salsa

This simple salsa is very easy to make, yet delicious. It is great with tortilla chips. For something a little different, try serving it on hearts of romaine lettuce or Green Plantain Chips (page 167).

Makes about 5 cups (1.25 L)

Tip

If you prefer, substitute 2 Mexican serrano chiles for the jalapeños.

2	mangos, diced (about 4 cups/1 L)	2
½ cup	finely diced red onion	125 mL
½	red bell pepper, diced	½
1	jalapeño pepper, seeded and minced (see Tip, left)	1
¼ cup	freshly squeezed lime juice	60 mL
1 tbsp	minced fresh mint leaves	15 mL

1. In a large bowl, combine mangos, red onion, bell pepper, jalapeño pepper, lime juice and mint. Toss well. Set aside for 10 minutes to meld flavors. Transfer to a serving bowl and serve.

Pineapple Mango Salsa

Vegan Friendly

For a simple presentation, serve this fruity salsa with tostadas or tortilla chips. If you're feeling more ambitious, make Green Plantain Chips (page 167). It even makes a nice finish for grilled chicken or shrimp.

Makes 8 cups (2 L)

Tips

The finer your dice, the smaller your dipper can be. If you are using small tortilla chips, err on the side of a fine dice.

If your fruit is not as sweet as you would like add 1 to 2 tsp (5 to 10 mL) sugar or agave syrup before mixing the salsa.

If you are vegan, be sure to use agave or unbleached organic sugar to ensure it has not been filtered through bone char.

1	pineapple, cored and diced (see Tips, left)	1
2	mangos, diced	2
1	small red onion, finely diced (about ⅓ cup/75 mL)	1
1	red bell pepper, finely diced	1
1	jalapeño pepper or 2 Mexican serrano chiles, seeded and minced	1
1 tbsp	finely chopped fresh cilantro leaves	15 mL
¼ tsp	puréed gingerroot (see Tips, page 120)	1 mL
	Granulated sugar or agave syrup, optional (see Tips, left)	
¼ cup	freshly squeezed lime juice	60 mL

1. In a large bowl, combine pineapple, mangos, red onion, bell pepper, jalapeño pepper, cilantro, ginger, and sugar, if using. Mix well. Add lime juice and toss well. Set aside for 10 minutes to meld flavors. Transfer to a serving bowl and serve.

Classic Mango Salsa

This salsa is wonderful and so darn easy to make. It's great with tortilla chips. For something a little different, try it as a finish for bite-sized salmon patties.

Makes about 1½ cups (375 mL)

Tips

A ripe mango is critical to this recipe. If you need to ripen a mango, here are a few tips: Place the mango at room temperature until it's soft to the touch and has a fruity smell. A quicker way to ripen the mango is to place it and an apple in a paper bag at room temperature. The apple will give off ethylene gas, which contributes to the ripening.

If you have a problem digesting gluten, substitute gluten-free tamari soy sauce for the traditional version.

1¼ cups	diced mango (see Tips, left)	300 mL
¼ cup	diced tomato	60 mL
1 tbsp	minced chives	15 mL
2 tsp	chiffonade fresh mint leaves	10 mL
1 tsp	light soy sauce (see Tips, left)	5 mL
1 tsp	sweet chili sauce	5 mL
1 tsp	freshly squeezed lime juice	5 mL

1. In a bowl, combine mango, tomato, chives, mint, soy sauce, chili sauce and lime juice. Cover and refrigerate for at least 1 hour to allow flavors to meld or for up to 8 hours before serving.

Mango Water Chestnut Salsa

The addition of water chestnuts puts an Asian spin on this tasty salsa. Continue that direction by serving it on thin slices of daikon radish, crisped in ice water and drained, or plain rice crackers.

	Makes about 4 cups (1 L)	

Tips

If you prefer, substitute a red finger chile for the jalapeño.

To purée peeled ginger: Use a fine, sharp-toothed grater such as Microplane.

1	mango, diced (about 2 cups/500 mL)	1
1	red bell pepper, finely diced	1
1	can (8 oz/227 mL) sliced water chestnuts, drained, rinsed and slivered	1
½	red onion, minced	½
1	jalapeño pepper, minced (see Tips, left)	1
¼ cup	freshly squeezed lime juice	60 mL
1 tbsp	freshly puréed gingerroot (see Tips, left)	15 mL

1. In a large bowl, combine mango, bell pepper, water chestnuts, red onion, jalapeño pepper, lime juice and ginger. Toss well. Set aside for 10 minutes to meld flavors. Transfer to a serving bowl and serve.

Margarita Mango Salsa

The addition of tequila to this salsa creates the perfect adults-only salsa. It's great with tortilla chips, but if you want to try something different, use it as a topping for bite-sized crab cakes or fish sticks.

Makes about 1¾ cups (425 mL)

Tip

There are numerous brands of tequila available. For the 1 tbsp (15 mL) called for in this recipe, feel free to use your favorite or what is readily available.

1½ cups	diced mango (see Tips, page 119)	375 mL
¼ cup	thinly sliced green onions, green part only	60 mL
1 tbsp	finely diced seeded jalapeño pepper	15 mL
1 tbsp	coarsely chopped fresh cilantro	15 mL
1 tsp	finely diced red bell pepper	5 mL
2 tbsp	freshly squeezed lime juice	30 mL
1 tbsp	tequila (see Tip, left)	15 mL

1. In a bowl, combine mango, green onions, jalapeño, cilantro, bell pepper, lime juice and tequila. Cover and refrigerate for at least 1 hour to allow flavors to meld or for up to 8 hours before serving.

Variation

If tequila is not available, vodka would make a fine substitute.

Thai-Inspired Green Mango Salsa

A wonderful accompaniment to any Thai-inspired meal. Good enough to be served on its own, with rice crackers, it can also be used as an accompaniment to appetizer satays.

Makes about 1¾ cups (425 mL)

Tip

There is a difference between rice vinegar and seasoned rice vinegar. Both are usually made from fermented rice or rice wine, but rice vinegar does not contain any additional sugar or sodium. Our preference is Japanese rice vinegar which is very mild flavored and almost colorless.

1½ cups	diced green mango	375 mL
¼ cup	roasted unsalted peanuts	60 mL
¼ cup	diced red onion	60 mL
5 tsp	rice vinegar (see Tip, left)	25 mL
1 tsp	finely diced red bell pepper	5 mL
1 tsp	coarsely chopped fresh cilantro	5 mL
¼ tsp	hot pepper flakes	1 mL
¼ tsp	agave syrup	1 mL

1. In a bowl, combine mango, peanuts, red onion, vinegar, bell pepper, cilantro, hot pepper flakes and agave syrup. Cover and refrigerate for at least 1 hour to allow flavors to meld or for up to 1 day before serving.

Apple Salsa

Try this wonderful salsa on top of a slice of Cheddar cheese.

Makes about 1¾ cups (425 mL)

Tip

Gala apples are light red in color with sweet, very mild apple flavor. Any crisp, sweet apple would be a great substitute.

1 cup	finely diced Gala apples (see Tip, left)	250 mL
¾ cup	finely diced Granny Smith apples	175 mL
⅓ cup	dried cranberries	75 mL
1 tbsp	finely diced shallots	15 mL
1 tbsp	Champagne vinegar or apple cider vinegar	15 mL
1 tsp	fig marmalade or other fruit marmalade	5 mL
¼ tsp	salt	1 mL
Pinch	ground cardamom	Pinch

1. In a bowl, combine Gala and Granny Smith apples, cranberries, shallots, vinegar, marmalade, salt and ground cardamom. Cover and refrigerate for at least 1 hour to allow flavors to meld or for up to 8 hours before serving.

Apple and Dried Cranberry Salsa

This salsa is almost like eating a piece of apple pie! It is wonderful on seared pork tenderloin medallions or on top of a slice of Cheddar cheese.

Makes about 1½ cups (375 mL)

Tip

When using any dried fruit, such as cranberries, choose versions that are sweetened with fruit juice rather than sugar.

1½ cups	finely diced peeled Granny Smith apples	375 mL
¼ cup	coarsely chopped dried cranberries (see Tip, left)	60 mL
2 tsp	Champagne vinegar or white wine	10 mL
1 tsp	packed brown sugar	5 mL
1 tsp	apricot jam or preserves	5 mL

1. In a bowl, combine apples, cranberries, vinegar, brown sugar and apricot jam. Cover and refrigerate for at least 1 hour to allow flavors to meld or for up to 8 hours before serving.

Cucumber Watermelon Salsa

Pass rice crackers, tortilla chips or Green Plantain Chips (page 167). This makes a very refreshing hot weather nibbly.

**Makes
4 cups (1 L)**

Tip

Agave syrup is produced from the agave plant and because it contains a high percentage of fructose it is much sweeter than honey. It is available in natural food stores. If you can't find it, substitute liquid honey. You may want to increase the quantity.

2 cups	diced seeded cucumber (about 1)	500 mL
2 cups	diced seeded watermelon	500 mL
16	fresh mint leaves (about 2 sprigs), finely chopped	16
1 tbsp	freshly squeezed orange juice	15 mL
1 tbsp	freshly squeezed lime juice	15 mL
2 tsp	light agave syrup (see Tip, left)	10 mL
1 tsp	finely minced seeded jalapeño pepper	5 mL
	Salt	

1. In a bowl, combine cucumber, watermelon, mint, orange juice, lime juice, agave syrup and jalapeño. Toss well to combine. Season to taste with salt. Cover and refrigerate for 30 minutes or for up to 4 hours to allow flavors to meld.

Feta-Spiked
Watermelon Salsa with Chile

You may think this is an unusual combination of ingredients, but watermelon, feta and chile are wildly compatible. Serve this with rice crackers or tortilla chips and expect to wow your guests. It is a fabulous hot-weather cooler.

**Makes about
4 cups (1 L)**

Tip

To toast pumpkin seeds: Place seeds in a dry skillet over medium heat and cook, stirring, until they begin to brown and pop, about 3 minutes. Immediately transfer to a small bowl.

4 cups	diced seeded watermelon	1 L
¼ cup	crumbled feta cheese	60 mL
2 tbsp	plain yogurt	30 mL
2 tbsp	finely chopped fresh cilantro leaves	30 mL
½ tsp	mild chile powder such as ancho, New Mexico or Aleppo	2 mL
2 tbsp	toasted pumpkin seeds (pepitas) (see Tip, left)	30 mL
	Salt	

1. In a bowl, combine watermelon, feta, yogurt, cilantro, chile powder and toasted pumpkin seeds. Toss well to combine. Season to taste with salt. Cover and refrigerate for 30 minutes or for up to 4 hours to allow flavors to meld.

Tropical Fruit Salsa

Vegan Friendly

Close your eyes and picture the sunshine and the ocean as you taste a real taste of the tropics atop a Green Plantain Chip (page 167). Tostadas or tortilla chips work well, too.

Makes about 1¼ cups (300 mL)

Tip

To remove vanilla seeds from pod: Using a sharp knife, slice pod lengthwise and using the back of the knife, gently scrape the pod to release the seeds.

½ cup	finely diced pineapple	125 mL
⅓ cup	finely diced kiwifruit	75 mL
¼ cup	finely diced mango	60 mL
¼ cup	grapefruit segments	60 mL
1 tsp	finely diced red bell pepper	5 mL
½ tsp	minced chives	2 mL
½ tsp	chopped fresh cilantro leaves	2 mL
¼ tsp	vanilla seeds (see Tip, left)	1 mL

1. In a bowl, combine pineapple, kiwi, mango, grapefruit, bell pepper, chives, cilantro and vanilla seeds. Cover and refrigerate for at least 1 hour to allow flavors to meld or for up to 1 day before serving.

Strawberry and Rhubarb Salsa

Vegan Friendly

This salsa is incredible when paired with a simple baked Brie or Basic Crostini (page 176).

(page 176).

Makes about 1 cup (250 mL)

Tip

Agave syrup is produced from the agave plant and because it contains a high percentage of fructose, it is much sweeter than honey.

1 cup	diced strawberries, divided	250 mL
1 cup	diced rhubarb	250 mL
½ cup	sweet white wine	125 mL
2	cardamom pods	2
½ cup	blueberries	125 mL
1 tbsp	agave syrup (see Tip, left)	15 mL
¼ tsp	finely chopped fresh thyme leaves	1 mL
⅛ tsp	finely chopped fresh mint leaves	0.5 mL
	Ground cardamom	

1. In a medium saucepan, bring ½ cup (125 mL) of the strawberries, rhubarb, white wine and cardamom pods to a boil over medium heat. Reduce heat and simmer, stirring often, until rhubarb is soft, 3 to 5 minutes. Strain mixture through a fine-mesh sieve, reserving liquid. Transfer solids to a bowl, discarding cardamom pods, and let cool. Return reserved cooking liquid to saucepan and bring to a simmer over medium-low heat. Simmer until reduced to a syrup, about 6 minutes. Add to reserved strawberry mixture in bowl.

2. Add remaining strawberries, blueberries, agave syrup, thyme, mint, and ground cardamom to taste and mix well. Serve immediately or cover and refrigerate for up to 2 days.

Jicama Strawberry Salsa

If you've never had a jicama you're missing out. The crunchy refreshing fruit pairs beautifully with the sweetness of strawberries and is perfect on top of apple and pear slices, crunchy Green Plantain Chips (page 167) or any sweet wonton.

Makes about 1½ cups (375 mL)

1½ cups	diced peeled jicama	375 mL
1 cup	diced strawberries	250 mL
¼ cup	Bing cherries, cut in half	60 mL
1 tbsp	extra virgin olive oil	15 mL
1 tbsp	balsamic vinegar	15 mL
1 tsp	agave syrup	5 mL
1 tsp	finely chopped fresh basil leaves	5 mL
⅛ tsp	salt	0.5 mL
Pinch	chipotle powder	Pinch

1. In a bowl, combine jicama, strawberries, cherries, olive oil, balsamic vinegar, agave syrup, basil, salt and chipotle powder. Cover and refrigerate for at least 1 hour to allow flavors to meld or for up to 8 hours before serving.

Spicy Nectarine Salsa

Here's an awesome and unique way to use this sweet stone fruit. Serve with Basic Crostini (page 176) for a delightful summertime appetizer or serve on top of peach slices — either way it's a salsa not to be missed.

Makes about 1½ cups (375 mL)

1¼ cups	diced nectarines	300 mL
3 tbsp	freshly squeezed lime juice	45 mL
1 tbsp	finely diced red onion	15 mL
1 tsp	chopped fresh cilantro leaves	5 mL
½ tsp	thinly sliced green onion	2 mL
¼ tsp	Asian chili sauce, such as sambal oelek	1 mL

1. In a bowl, combine nectarines, lime juice, red onion, cilantro, green onion and chili sauce. Cover and refrigerate for at least 1 hour to allow flavors to meld or for up to 8 hours before serving.

Bean Dips, Spreads and Salsas

Basil and White Bean Spread

If you don't tell, no one will ever guess how easy it is to make this delicious and sophisticated spread. Serve this with sliced baguette or crackers or use as a topping for Basic Crostini (page 176). You'll need about 24 crostini.

Makes about 3 cups (750 mL)

Tips

For this quantity of beans, use 1 can (14 to 19 oz/ 398 to 540 mL) beans, drained and rinsed, or cook 1 cup (250 mL) dried beans.

We always use flat-leaf rather than curly parsley because it has more flavor.

• **Food processor**

2 cups	cooked drained white kidney (cannellini) beans (see Tips, left)	500 mL
2 cups	packed Italian flat-leaf parsley leaves (see Tips, left)	500 mL
2 tbsp	basil pesto	30 mL
4	cloves garlic, coarsely chopped	4
1 tbsp	extra virgin olive oil	15 mL
1 tbsp	freshly squeezed lemon juice	15 mL
	Salt and freshly ground black pepper	

1. In food processor fitted with metal blade, process beans, parsley, basil pesto, garlic, olive oil and lemon juice until smooth, about 1 minute. Season to taste with salt and pepper. Transfer to a serving bowl. Serve immediately or cover and refrigerate for up to 2 days. If refrigerated, before serving, let stand at room temperature for about 20 minutes to allow the flavors to develop.

Chive and Navy Bean Dip

Raw chives add a wonderful peppery note to the navy beans. This dip is perfect with crisp tortilla chips or Beet Chips (page 169).

Tip

If you have difficulty digesting beans, cook dried beans from scratch. Add 1 tbsp (15 mL) lemon juice to the soaking water. Discard the soaking water and rinse well before cooking.

- **Food processor**

¼ cup	extra virgin olive oil	60 mL
1⅓ cups	cooked white navy beans (see Tip, left)	325 mL
1¼ cups	coarsely chopped fresh chives	300 mL
¼ cup	raw peanuts	60 mL
1 tsp	salt	5 mL
1 tsp	sherry vinegar	5 mL

1. In a saucepan, heat oil over medium heat. Add beans, chives and peanuts and cook, stirring, until chives are bright green and soft, 3 to 5 minutes. Remove from heat. Add salt and vinegar. Transfer to food processor fitted with metal blade and pulse until smooth. Transfer to a serving bowl. Serve immediately or cover and refrigerate for up to 3 days.

Cauliflower and Lentil Hummus Spiked with Cumin

The next time you're having a party, try this deliciously different variation on the theme of hummus. This makes a big batch but can easily be halved. Serve with warm pita bread.

Makes about 4 cups (1 L)

Tips

For this quantity of lentils, use 1 can (14 to 19 oz/ 398 to 540 mL) drained rinsed lentils or cook 1 cup (250 mL) dry lentils.

For best flavor, toast and grind cumin seeds yourself. *To toast seeds:* Place seeds in a dry skillet over medium heat, and cook, stirring, until fragrant, about 3 minutes. Immediately transfer to a mortar or a spice grinder and grind.

Aleppo chiles are Syrian in origin. They are moderately hot and quite fruity and lend pleasant authenticity to recipes with a Middle Eastern slant. A smaller quantity of cayenne will produce a similar amount of heat.

• **Food processor**

4 cups	cauliflower florets (1 small head), cooked and drained	1 L
2 cups	cooked drained brown or green lentils (see Tips, left)	500 mL
½ cup	extra virgin olive oil (approx.)	125 mL
⅓ cup	tahini	75 mL
¼ cup	freshly squeezed lemon juice	60 mL
6	green onions, white part with a bit of green, cut into chunks	6
½ cup	Italian flat-leaf parsley leaves	125 mL
4	cloves garlic, coarsely chopped	4
1 tbsp	ground cumin (see Tips, left)	15 mL
2 tsp	ground Aleppo pepper or ½ tsp (2 mL) cayenne pepper (see Tips, left)	10 mL
1 tsp	salt	5 mL
	Freshly ground black pepper	

1. In food processor fitted with metal blade, process cooked cauliflower, lentils, olive oil, tahini and lemon juice until smooth, about 30 seconds, stopping and scraping down sides of the bowl as necessary. If necessary, add 1 to 2 tbsp (15 to 30 mL) of olive oil and pulse to blend. (You want the mixture to be quite creamy.)

2. Add green onions, parsley, garlic, cumin, Aleppo pepper, salt, and black pepper to taste and process until smooth, about 15 seconds. Taste and adjust garlic, lemon juice and/or salt to suit your taste. Process again, if necessary.

3. Transfer to a serving bowl. Serve immediately or refrigerate for up to 1 day. If refrigerated, before serving, let stand at room temperature for about 20 minutes to allow the flavors to develop.

Down-Home Hummus

If you're a fan of hummus but are getting tired of the same old thing, try this variation on the theme. Black-eyed peas, peanuts and peanut butter stand in for chickpeas and tahini. Green bell pepper and sweet onion complete the Southern spin on this tasty and nutritious spread. Serve with crudités or warm pita bread.

**Makes
3 cups (750 mL)**

Tips

For this quantity of black-eyed peas, use 1 can (14 to 19 oz/398 to 540 mL) drained and rinsed or cook 1 cup (250 mL) dried chickpeas.

If you have cooked the peas yourself, scoop out about 1 cup (250 mL) of the cooking water before draining and set aside.

• **Food processor**

1	green bell pepper, chopped	1
½ cup	roasted peanuts	125 mL
½	sweet onion, such as Vidalia or red onion, quartered	½
2	cloves garlic (approx.)	2
2 cups	cooked drained black-eyed peas (see Tips, left)	500 mL
2 tbsp	peanut butter	30 mL
2 tbsp	warm water or bean cooking water (approx.) (see Tips, left)	30 mL
2 tbsp	freshly squeezed lemon juice	30 mL
2 tbsp	extra virgin olive oil	30 mL
1 tsp	salt	5 mL
½ tsp	freshly ground black pepper	2 mL
¼ tsp	hot pepper sauce	1 mL

1. In food processor fitted with metal blade, pulse bell pepper, peanuts, onion and garlic until finely chopped, about 10 times. Add peas, peanut butter, water, lemon juice, olive oil, salt, black pepper and hot pepper sauce and process until smooth, about 30 seconds, stopping and scraping down sides of the bowl as necessary. If necessary, add additional warm water and pulse to blend. (You want the mixture to be quite creamy.) Taste and adjust lemon juice, garlic and/or hot sauce to suit your taste. Process again, if necessary.

2. Transfer to a serving bowl. Serve immediately or cover and refrigerate for up to 1 day. If refrigerated, before serving, let stand at room temperature for about 20 minutes to allow the flavors to develop.

Easy Hummus

Use as both a dip and a spread. Serve with crudités or Pita Chips (see Variations, page 173) or as a condiment for falafels.

Makes about 1½ cups (375 mL)

Tips

We prefer to use no-salt-added chickpeas, which are usually available in organic or natural food sections in large grocery stores or fine food shops.

For this quality of chickpeas, use 1 can (14 to 19 oz/398 to 540 mL), drained and rinsed or cook 1 cup (250 mL) dried chickpeas.

• Food processor

½ cup	water	125 mL
3	cloves garlic	3
2 cups	canned chickpeas, drained and rinsed (see Tips, left)	500 mL
¼ tsp	ground cumin (see Tips, page 138)	1 mL
½ tsp	hot pepper sauce	2 mL
1 tbsp	extra virgin olive oil	15 mL
1 tsp	salt	5 mL

1. In a medium saucepan, bring water and garlic to a boil over high heat. Reduce heat and boil gently until water is fully evaporated, about 10 minutes. Add chickpeas and cover and cook until chickpeas are tender to the touch, about 5 minutes. Add cumin, hot pepper sauce, olive oil and salt. Transfer to food processor and purée until smooth, about 30 seconds, stopping and scraping down sides of the bowl as necessary. If hummus is too thick, add warm water to reach desired consistency.

Variation

Roasted Eggplant with Hummus: Cut 1 eggplant into ½-inch (1 cm) thick slices. Brush with olive oil and bake in a 400°F (200°C) oven for about 25 minutes. Top with hummus.

Hummus from Scratch

Although it's more work, cooking dried chickpeas rather than using canned chickpeas produces the tastiest hummus. Try this and see if you agree. Warm pita or Crisp Pita Bread (page 172) is a favorite accompaniment, but it's also good with crudités. Hummus also makes a great sauce for grilled kabobs, particularly lamb and a great topping for roasted eggplant (see Variation, page 136).

Makes about 3 cups (750 mL)

Tips

If you're in a hurry, instead of setting the chickpeas aside to soak, cover the pot and bring to a boil. Boil for 3 minutes. Turn off heat and soak for 1 hour. Drain and rinse thoroughly with cold water. Then proceed with cooking as in Step 2.

For added flavor, when cooking the chickpeas (Step 2), add garlic, bay leaves or a bouquet garni made from your favorite herbs tied together in a cheesecloth bag.

- **Food processor**

1 cup	dried chickpeas (see Tips, left)	250 mL
1/3 cup	tahini	75 mL
1/3 cup	extra virgin olive oil	75 mL
1/4 cup	freshly squeezed lemon juice	60 mL
1/4 cup	Italian flat-leaf parsley leaves	60 mL
2	cloves garlic (approx.)	2
1 tsp	ground cumin (see Tips, page 138)	5 mL
1 tsp	salt (approx.)	5 mL
1/2 tsp	freshly ground black pepper	2 mL
1/4 tsp	cayenne pepper, optional	1 mL
	Sweet paprika, optional	

1. In a large saucepan, combine chickpeas and 3 cups (750 mL) cold water. Set aside to soak for at least 6 hours or overnight. Drain and rinse thoroughly with cold water.

2. Return drained chickpeas to saucepan and add 3 cups (750 mL) cold fresh water. Cover and bring to a boil over medium-high heat. Reduce heat and simmer until chickpeas are tender, about 1 hour. Scoop out about 1 cup (250 mL) of cooking water and set aside. Drain and rinse chickpeas.

3. In food processor fitted with metal blade, process cooked chickpeas, tahini, olive oil, 1/4 cup (60 mL) of the cooking water and lemon juice until smooth, about 30 seconds, stopping and scraping down sides of the bowl as necessary. If necessary, add additional cooking water and pulse to blend. (You want the mixture to be quite creamy.) Add parsley, garlic, cumin, salt, pepper, and cayenne, if using, and process until smooth, about 15 seconds. Taste and adjust garlic, lemon juice and/or salt to suit your taste. Process again, if necessary. Spoon into a serving bowl and dust with paprika, if using.

Oil-Poached Garlic Hummus

Poached garlic in olive oil imparts the most delicate sweet garlic flavor you've ever tasted. Parsnip Chips (page 171) would be great with this hummus and pita bread always makes a good accompaniment.

Makes about 1½ cups (375 mL)

Tips

For best flavor, toast and grind cumin yourself.

To toast seeds: Place seeds in a dry skillet over medium heat and cook, stirring, until fragrant about 3 minutes. Immediately transfer to a mortar or a spice grinder and grind.

Garlic-flavored oil is wonderful to cook with and is even perfect in vinaigrettes. It should be kept refrigerated for up to 1 week only and then discarded.

• Food processor

2 cups	extra virgin olive oil	500 mL
½ cup	garlic cloves	125 mL
½ cup	water	125 mL
2 cups	cooked chickpeas, rinsed and drained (see Tips, page 139)	500 mL
1 tsp	grated lemon zest	10 mL
1 tbsp	freshly squeezed lemon juice	15 mL
½ tsp	salt	2 mL
¼ tsp	ground cumin (see Tips, left)	1 mL

1. In a medium saucepan over medium heat, bring olive oil and garlic to a simmer. Reduce heat to keep oil hot, but not simmering, and poach until garlic is soft, 15 to 20 minutes. Be sure to watch closely and adjust the temperature to avoid burning, which will impart a very bitter flavor. Using a slotted spoon, transfer garlic to a bowl and set aside. Reserve the olive oil.

2. In another medium saucepan, bring water to a boil over high heat. Add chickpeas and cover until chickpeas are very soft and hot. Drain and transfer to food processor. Add poached garlic, lemon zest and juice, salt, cumin and ¼ cup (60 mL) of the reserved olive oil and purée until smooth, about 30 seconds, stopping and scraping down sides of the bowl as necessary. If hummus is too thick, add warm water to reach desired consistency. Serve immediately or refrigerate for up to 3 days.

Roasted Red Pepper Hummus

This subtle twist on a classic dip is wonderful when spread on wedges of sweet bell pepper. It is also delicious with warm pita bread.

Makes about 1¾ cups (425 mL)

Tips

For this quality of chickpeas, use 1 can (14 to 19 oz/398 to 540 mL), drained and rinsed or cook 1 cup (250 mL) dried chickpeas.

For best flavor, toast and grind cumin seeds yourself. *To toast seeds:* Place seeds in a dry skillet over medium heat, and cook, stirring, until fragrant, about 3 minutes. Immediately transfer to a mortar or a spice grinder and grind.

- **Preheat oven to 300°F (150°C)**
- **Food processor**

1	red bell pepper	1
2 tbsp	extra virgin olive oil	30 mL
½ cup	water	125 mL
3	cloves garlic	3
2 cups	cooked chickpeas, drained and rinsed (see Tips, left)	500 mL
½ tsp	hot pepper sauce	2 mL
½ tsp	salt	2 mL
¼ tsp	ground cumin (see Tips, left)	1 mL

1. Rub bell pepper with oil to fully coat. Place in a baking dish and roast in preheated oven until skin is blistered but pepper still maintains its shape, about 45 minutes. Let cool. Over a bowl, using a strainer, peel and remove stem and seeds. Reserve residual liquid.

2. In a medium saucepan, bring water and garlic to a boil over high heat. Reduce heat and boil gently until water is fully evaporated, about 10 minutes. Add chickpeas and cover and cook until chickpeas are tender to the touch, about 5 minutes. Drain chickpeas and transfer to a food processor.

3. Add roasted pepper with reserved liquid, hot pepper sauce, salt and cumin and purée until smooth, about 30 seconds, stopping and scraping down sides of the bowl as necessary. If hummus is too thick, add warm water to reach desired consistency.

Hot and Smoky Bean Dip

Served bubbling hot, this cheesy dip with just a hint of spice and smoke makes a great cold weather treat. Serve with tortilla chips, tostadas or sliced baguette.

Makes about 3 cups (750 mL)

Tips

For this quality of black-eyed peas, use 1 can (14 to 19 oz/ 398 to 540 mL), drained and rinsed or cook 1 cup (250 mL) dried black-eyed peas.

To roast peppers: Preheat broiler. Place pepper(s) on a baking sheet and broil, turning two or three times, until skin on all sides is blackened, about 25 minutes. Transfer to a heatproof bowl. Cover with a plate and let stand until cool. Remove and, using a sharp knife, lift skins off. Discard skins, core and seeds.

- **Preheat oven to 350°F (180°C)**
- **Food processor**

2 cups	cooked drained black-eyed peas (see Tips, left)	500 mL
1	roasted red pepper (see Tips, left)	1
2	green onions, white part with a bit of green, cut into chunks	2
2 tbsp	drained chopped pickled hot banana peppers	30 mL
1 to 2 tsp	smoked paprika	5 to 10 mL
2 cups	shredded Cheddar cheese	500 mL
¼ cup	mayonnaise	60 mL
¼ cup	sour cream	60 mL

1. In food processor fitted with metal blade, pulse peas, roasted pepper, green onions, banana peppers and paprika until chopped and blended, about 20 times. Add cheese, mayonnaise and sour cream and process until desired texture is achieved. Transfer to an ovenproof serving dish and bake in preheated oven until hot and bubbling, about 20 minutes.

Lemon-Laced Butterbean Dip

Vegan Friendly

Delicious and healthful, this Mediterranean-inspired dip is very easy to make. Serve it with Crisp Pita Bread (page 172), sliced baguette or crudités.

Makes about 1 cup (250 mL)

Tips

To soak lima beans: Bring dried beans to a boil in 6 cups (1.5 L) water over medium heat. Boil rapidly for 3 minutes. Cover, turn off element and let stand for 1 hour. Drain.

We always use flat-leaf rather than curly parsley because it has more flavor.

• **Food processor**

1 cup	dried lima beans, soaked (see Tips, left)	250 mL
¼ cup	freshly squeezed lemon juice	60 mL
¼ cup	extra virgin olive oil	60 mL
1 tsp	salt	5 mL
	Freshly ground black pepper	
½ cup	loosely packed Italian flat-leaf parsley leaves	125 mL
4	green onions, white part only, cut into chunks	4

1. In a large pot of water, cook soaked beans until tender, about 30 minutes. Scoop out about 1 cup (250 mL) of the cooking liquid and set aside. Drain beans, rinse under cold running water and pop out of their skins. Discard skins.

2. In food processor fitted with metal blade, pulse cooked beans, lemon juice, olive oil, salt, and pepper to taste until blended, about 5 times. Gradually add just enough bean cooking water through the feed tube to make a smooth emulsion, pulsing to blend, about 10 times. Add parsley and green onions and pulse until chopped and integrated, about 5 times.

3. Transfer to a serving bowl. Cover and refrigerate for up to 2 days or until ready to use.

Santorini-Style Fava Spread

This spread, which is Greek in origin, is unusual and particularly delicious. Although fava beans do figure in Greek cuisine, for most Greek people fava is synonymous with yellow split peas, one of the major indigenous foods of the island of Santorini, from which they make many dishes, including variations of this spread. Serve this with warm toasted pita and wait for the compliments.

Makes about 2 cups (500 mL)

Tip

Italian flat-leaf parsley is preferred because it has much more flavor than the curly leaf variety.

- **Small (1½ to 2 quart) slow cooker**
- **Food processor**

½ cup	extra virgin olive oil, divided	125 mL
½ cup	diced shallots (about 2 large)	125 mL
2 tsp	dried oregano	10 mL
1 tsp	salt	5 mL
½ tsp	cracked black peppercorns	2 mL
1 cup	yellow split peas	250 mL
4 cups	water	1 L
6	oil-packed sun-dried tomato halves, drained and coarsely chopped	6
4	cloves garlic, chopped	4
¼ cup	coarsely chopped Italian flat-leaf parsley (see Tip, left)	60 mL
4	fresh basil leaves, hand-torn	4
3 tbsp	red wine vinegar	45 mL
	Salt and freshly ground black pepper	
	Toasted pita bread	

1. In a skillet, heat 1 tbsp (15 mL) of the oil over medium heat. Add shallots and cook, stirring, until softened, about 3 minutes. Add oregano, salt and peppercorns and cook, stirring, for 1 minute. Add split peas and cook, stirring, until coated. Add water and bring to a boil. Boil for 2 minutes.

Make Ahead

Complete Step 1. Cover and refrigerate for up to 2 days. When you're ready to serve, heat peas on the stovetop until bubbles form about the edges. Complete the recipe.

2. Transfer to slow cooker stoneware. Cover and cook on Low for 8 hours or on High for 4 hours, until peas have virtually disintegrated. Drain off excess water, if necessary. Transfer solids to food processor. Add sun-dried tomatoes, garlic, parsley, basil and vinegar. Pulse 7 or 8 times to chop and blend ingredients. With motor running, add remaining olive oil in a steady stream through the feed tube. Season to taste with additional salt and pepper and drizzle with additional olive oil, if desired. Serve warm with toasted pita.

Roasted Cubanelle Pepper and Black Bean Salsa

Cubanelle peppers combined with chipotle powder create a wonderfully smoky salsa that is just delightful with tortilla chips or Green Plantain Chips (page 167).

Makes about 2 cups (500 mL)

Tip

Cubanelle peppers are long, narrow sweet peppers with a very mild flavor. These peppers are green to yellow in color when unripe and bright red when fully ripe.

1 cup	diced peeled grilled Cubanelle pepper (see Tip, left)	250 mL
½ cup	cooked drained black beans (see Tips, page 147)	125 mL
¼ cup	finely diced cherry tomatoes	60 mL
3 tbsp	freshly squeezed lime juice	45 mL
2 tbsp	coarsely chopped fresh cilantro leaves	30 mL
⅛ tsp	chipotle powder	0.5 mL
⅛ tsp	ancho chile powder	0.5 mL
Pinch	salt	Pinch

1. In a bowl, combine Cubanelle peppers, black beans, tomatoes, lime juice, cilantro, chipotle powder, ancho powder and salt. Serve immediately or cover and refrigerate for up to 1 day.

Black Bean and Salsa Dip

This tasty Cuban-inspired dip can be made from ingredients you're likely to have on hand. Serve with tortilla chips, tostadas, crisp crackers or crudités. If you are looking for a finish with more pizzazz, try Fresh Corn Cakes (page 166), or one of the arepas (pages 179 and 180).

Makes about 3 cups (750 mL)

Tips

For this quantity of beans, soak, cook and drain 1 cup (250 mL) dried black beans or drain and rinse 1 can (14 to 19 oz/398 to 540 mL) black beans.

For a smoother dip, purée the beans in a food processor or mash with a potato masher before adding to stoneware.

If you use a five-alarm salsa in this dip, you may find it too spicy with the addition of jalapeño pepper.

If you don't have time to roast your own pepper, use a bottled roasted red pepper.

• Small (maximum 3½ quart) slow cooker

2 cups	cooked black beans (see Tips, left)	500 mL
8 oz	cream cheese, cubed	250 g
½ cup	tomato salsa	125 mL
¼ cup	sour cream	60 mL
2 tsp	cumin seeds, toasted and ground (see Tips, page 138)	10 mL
1 tsp	chili powder	5 mL
1 tsp	cracked black peppercorns	5 mL
1	jalapeño pepper, finely chopped, optional (see Tips, left)	1
1	roasted red bell pepper, finely chopped, optional (see Tips, page 140)	1
	Finely chopped green onion, optional	
	Finely chopped cilantro leaves, optional	

1. In slow cooker stoneware, combine beans, cream cheese, salsa, sour cream, cumin, chili powder, peppercorns, jalapeño pepper and roasted pepper, if using. Cover and cook on High for 1 hour. Stir again and cook on High for an additional 30 minutes, until mixture is hot and bubbly. Serve immediately or set temperature at Low until ready to serve. Garnish with green onion and/or cilantro, if desired.

Avocado Black Bean Salsa

In addition to being very tasty, this salsa is highly nutritious. Serve it on tostadas or tortilla chips, or use hearts of romaine lettuce as a dipper.

Makes about 3 cups (750 mL)

Tip

To prevent oxidization, don't dice your avocados until you have completed the rest of the chopping. Once diced, add to remaining ingredients and toss immediately.

2	avocados, diced (see Tip, left)	2
1 cup	diced peeled tomatoes	250 mL
1 cup	cooked drained black beans	250 mL
1	poblano pepper, seeded and diced	1
½ cup	finely diced red onion	125 mL
½	jalapeño pepper, seeded and diced	½
¼ cup	freshly squeezed lime juice	60 mL
2 tbsp	freshly squeezed orange juice	30 mL
1 tsp	puréed garlic	5 mL
2 tbsp	finely chopped fresh cilantro leaves	30 mL
	Salt and freshly ground black pepper	

1. In a bowl, combine avocados, tomatoes, beans, poblano pepper, red onion, jalapeño pepper, lime juice, orange juice, garlic and cilantro leaves. Toss well to combine. Season to taste with salt and black pepper. Cover and refrigerate for 30 minutes to allow flavors to meld.

Navy Bean Salsa

This salsa is packed full of flavor, so much so you may just be tempted to eat it all by itself. If behaving yourself, crunchy tortilla chips are all you need for a perfect finish.

Makes about 2 cups (500 mL)

Tips

Cook dried beans from scratch or used drained, rinsed canned beans. 1 cup (250 mL) dried beans makes 2 cups (500 mL) cooked.

If you don't have Pommery mustard, substitute an equal quantity of Dijon.

1¼ cups	cooked drained navy beans (see Tips, left)	300 mL
⅓ cup	finely diced celery	75 mL
¼ cup	finely diced carrot	60 mL
2 tbsp	finely diced red onion	30 mL
2 tbsp	finely diced bell pepper	30 mL
1 tbsp	thinly sliced green onions	15 mL

Vinaigrette

3 tbsp	sherry vinegar	45 mL
2 tbsp	extra virgin olive oil	30 mL
1 tbsp	grainy (Pommery) mustard (see Tips, left)	15 mL
1 tsp	herbes de Provence	5 mL
½ tsp	salt	2 mL
¼ tsp	freshly cracked peppercorns	1 mL

1. In a bowl, combine beans, celery, carrot, red onion, bell pepper and green onions.
2. *Vinaigrette:* In another bowl, combine vinegar, olive oil, mustard, herbes de Provence, salt and pepper. Whisk well to emulsify. Stir into vegetables and mix well. Serve immediately or cover and refrigerate for up to 1 day.

Kidney Bean Salsa

Bean salsas are so wonderful they can almost be eaten all on their own, but where's the fun in that? Dip tortilla chips or Bagel Chips (page 177) into the salsa and munch away.

Makes about 2 cups (500 mL)

Tip

To grill corn: Preheat barbecue grill to High. Grill ears of corn, husks on, rotating often until dark brown all over, about 20 minutes. Transfer to a plate and let cool for 5 minutes or until cool enough to handle. Remove husk and silks and using a serrated knife, cut kernels from cob.

1¼ cups	cooked drained kidney beans	300 mL
⅓ cup	grilled corn kernels (see Tip, left)	75 mL
¼ cup	coarsely chopped cherry tomatoes	60 mL
2 tbsp	finely diced sweet onion	30 mL
1 tbsp	thinly sliced green onions	15 mL

Vinaigrette

3 tbsp	red wine vinegar	45 mL
2 tbsp	extra virgin olive oil	30 mL
1 tbsp	thinly sliced fresh garlic	15 mL
1 tsp	Dijon mustard	5 mL
½ tsp	kosher salt	2 mL
¼ tsp	sambal (hot chile sauce)	1 mL

1. In a large bowl, combine kidney beans, corn, cherry tomatoes, onion and green onions.

2. *Vinaigrette:* In a separate bowl, combine vinegar, olive oil, garlic, Dijon, salt and chile sauce and whisk well to emulsify.

3. Stir vinaigrette into vegetables and mix well. Serve immediately or cover and refrigerate for up to 1 day.

Edamame Salsa

Edamame (also known as soy beans) are delicious and quite good for you, too. Plunge an endive spear or romaine leaf into the salsa to serve the perfect vegan appetizer.

Makes about 1 cup (250 mL)

Tip

To get the most juice from a lemon, it's best to use room temperature ones. (In a pinch, you can microwave a lemon on low for a few seconds to warm it slightly, which will "relax" it and make it easier to work with.) Before juicing, roll the lemon firmly on a counter back and forth for a few seconds to break the small interior membranes. This will make it easier to extract the juice.

¾ cup	frozen shelled edamame beans, thawed	175 mL
¼ cup	diced cucumber	60 mL
1 tsp	grated lemon zest	5 mL
1 tbsp	freshly squeezed lemon juice (see Tip, left)	15 mL
1 tsp	extra virgin olive oil	5 mL
1 tsp	thinly sliced red chile pepper	5 mL
½ tsp	minced garlic	2 mL
¼ tsp	salt	1 mL

1. In a pot of boiling salted water, boil edamame until tender, about 2 minutes. Drain and rinse under cold water until chilled. Drain well and transfer to a bowl.

2. Add cucumber, lemon zest and juice, olive oil, chile pepper, garlic and salt to edamame and mix well. Let stand at room temperature for at least 1 hour to allow flavors to meld or cover and refrigerate for up to 1 day before serving.

Desserts

Blueberry and Yogurt Dip

This is perfect with fruit skewers or fresh peach or apple wedges. Use the leftovers on your breakfast cereal.

| Makes about 1½ cups (375 mL) | | |

Tip

When serving cold dips, particularly those that contain a high proportion of dairy, consider lining a deep platter with crushed ice and use it to surround the bowl. Arranging crudités over the ice will help to keep them nicely chilled as well.

- **Blender**

⅔ cup	blueberries	150 mL
½ cup	water	125 mL
2 tbsp	agave syrup	30 mL
1 cup	plain yogurt	250 mL
½ tsp	grated lemon zest	2 mL
¼ tsp	vanilla extract	1 mL

1. In a saucepan, combine blueberries, water and agave and bring to a boil over medium heat. Reduce heat and boil gently until liquid is reduced by one-quarter. Transfer to a blender or use an immersion blender and purée until smooth.

2. Transfer to a bowl and let cool to room temperature. Fold in yogurt, lemon zest and vanilla until smooth. Serve immediately or cover and refrigerate for up to 3 days.

Variation

Try crème fraîche or sour cream in place of yogurt in this recipe. They impart a tasty sour note.

Champagne and Raspberry Dip

Each bite is like a delightful sip of a Kir Royale. Serve this dip next to a bowl of fresh strawberries for dipping and a glass of Champagne for an excellent brunch or dessert offering.

Makes about 1½ cups (375 mL)

Tips

If Champagne or Prosecco are not available or to your liking, feel free to substitute your favorite white wine.

If you are a vegetarian, use unbleached organic sugar to ensure it has not been filtered through bone char.

• **Blender**

½ cup	Champagne or Prosecco (see Tips, left)	125 mL
1 tbsp	granulated sugar (see Tips, left)	15 mL
½ cup	golden or red raspberries	125 mL
1 tsp	apricot jam	5 mL
1	fresh basil leaf	1
½ cup	whipped cream	125 mL

1. In a saucepan, bring Champagne and sugar to a boil over medium heat. Reduce heat and boil gently until reduced by three-quarters, about 5 minutes. Remove from heat. Add raspberries, jam and basil leaf. Transfer to a blender or use an immersion blender and purée until smooth. Let cool to room temperature.

2. Fold whipped cream, one-third at a time, into raspberry mixture and serve immediately.

Fig Yogurt Dip

This dip is perfect for fresh cut apples or pears (see Tips, left), or strawberries.

Makes about 1½ cups (375 mL)

Tips

Don't cut apples or pears too far ahead of time because they will turn brown. To prevent this from happening, after slicing, immerse in acidulated water (about 1 tbsp/15 mL) lemon juice to 4 cups (1 L) water), and refrigerate until you are ready to serve.

We prefer to use full-fat or whole milk yogurt in this recipe because it has a deeper flavor profile but if you prefer, use a lower-fat alternative.

Fig purée can be found in most gourmet shops and sometimes in large supermarkets.

1 cup	plain yogurt (see Tips, left)	250 mL
2 tbsp	fig purée (see Tips, left)	30 mL
1 tbsp	packed brown sugar	15 mL
1 tbsp	pure maple syrup	15 mL
1 tbsp	grated lemon zest	15 mL
1 tbsp	freshly squeezed lemon juice	15 mL

1. In a bowl, combine yogurt, fig purée, brown sugar, maple syrup, lemon zest and juice. Cover and refrigerate for 1 hour before serving or store for up to 3 days.

Mango Dip

Close your eyes and take a bite...off to the tropics you go! Enjoy with fresh cut fruit, sweet wontons, or simple, good-quality wafers.

Makes about 1¾ cups (425 mL)

Tips

The simplest way to peel a mango is with a vegetable peeler. Use a paring knife to cut away the flesh from the pit.

If you are a vegetarian, use unbleached organic sugar to ensure it has not been filtered through bone char.

• Blender

1 cup	chopped mango (see Tips, left)	250 mL
1 cup	water	250 mL
1 tbsp	granulated sugar (see Tips, left)	15 mL
1 tsp	coarsely chopped fresh mint leaves	5 mL
½ tsp	Champagne vinegar or apple cider vinegar	2 mL
1 cup	whipped cream	250 mL

1. In a saucepan, bring mango, water and sugar to a boil over medium heat. Reduce heat to low and simmer until liquid is reduced by half and mango is very soft, about 8 minutes. Add mint and vinegar. Transfer to a blender or use an immersion blender and purée until smooth. Transfer to a bowl and let cool to room temperature.

2. Fold whipped cream, one-third at a time, into mango purée and refrigerate for at least 1 hour before serving.

Warm Apple Sour Cream

Caution: highly addictive! This is the perfect dessert dip. Serve with fresh strawberries, apple, pear or pineapple wedges.

Makes about 1½ cups (375 mL)

Tip

Spread ¼ cup (60 mL) of dip in the middle of a plate to make a wonderful base for warm apple pie.

• **Food processor**

2 cups	chopped Granny Smith apples	500 mL
1 tbsp	freshly squeezed lemon juice	15 mL
1 tbsp	unsweetened apple juice or water	15 mL
1 tbsp	unsalted butter	15 mL
¾ cup	sour cream, at room temperature	175 mL
1 tsp	coarsely chopped fresh mint leaves	5 mL
⅛ tsp	salt	0.5 mL

1. In a saucepan, combine apples, lemon juice, apple juice and butter and bring to a simmer over medium heat. Reduce heat and boil gently until apples are breaking down, about 10 minutes. Transfer to a food processor and purée until smooth.

2. Transfer to a bowl and let cool. Stir in sour cream, mint and salt until smooth. Serve immediately.

Warm Banana Salsa

Why not try a dessert appetizer party? This salsa makes a wonderful finish for prepared desserts such as sweet wontons or chocolate wafers.

**Makes about
1 cup (250 mL)**

Tip

Agave syrup is produced from the agave plant and because it contains a high percentage of fructose, it is much sweeter than honey.

¼ tsp	sesame seeds	1 mL
¼ cup	finely diced dried apricots	60 mL
1¼ cups	diced bananas	300 mL
1 tsp	agave syrup (see Tip, left)	5 mL
1 tsp	freshly squeezed lemon juice	5 mL

1. Preheat a large skillet over medium heat until hot. Add sesame seeds and toast, stirring often, until slightly brown, about 3 minutes. Add apricots and cook, stirring, until warmed through, about 2 minutes. Add bananas, agave syrup and lemon juice. Stir to combine. Transfer to a bowl and serve warm or let cool to room temperature.

Date and Tamarind Chutney

This Indian-inspired treat is lusciously delicious. It's amazing served with slightly sweet crackers, such as fruit and nut crisps or British-type oat biscuits.

Makes about 1½ cups (375 mL)

Tip

Some brands of tamarind purée contain pieces of pits. If you notice pits in yours, strain through a fine sieve after soaking.

- **Food processor**

1 cup	hot water	250 mL
1 tsp	Demerara or other raw cane sugar	5 mL
2 oz	unsalted Thai tamarind purée, broken into pieces (about 2 tbsp/30 mL) (see Tip, left)	60 g
8 oz	pitted soft dates such as medjool (about 1 cup/250 mL)	250 g
1	long red chile pepper, seeded and coarsely chopped	1
½ tsp	ground cumin (see Tips, page 138)	2 mL

1. In a small bowl, combine hot water and sugar. Stir well until sugar is dissolved. Add tamarind and set aside for 30 minutes.

2. In food processor fitted with metal blade, process dates, chile pepper, cumin and tamarind mixture until smooth and creamy, about 1 minute. Add water, if necessary, and pulse to create a smooth texture. Serve immediately or cover and refrigerate in an airtight container for up to 1 week.

Chocolate Mousse Spread

Surprise pop-in guests with an elegant and fun dessert canapé of your favorite cookie topped with a small dollop of Chocolate Mousse Spread and some shaved chocolate curls.

Makes about 1¼ cups (300 mL)

Tips

Fresh fruits, such as strawberries, mango, apples and pineapple, or even a beautiful wafer, would all be wonderful plunged into this dip.

If you are a vegetarian, use unbleached organic sugar to ensure it has not been filtered through bone char.

¾ cup	heavy or whipping (35%) cream	175 mL
1 tbsp	granulated sugar (see Tips, left)	15 mL
⅓ cup	semisweet chocolate chips	75 mL
1 tbsp	unsalted butter, finely diced	15 mL

1. In a bowl, using an electric mixer or whisk, beat cream and sugar to stiff peaks. Set aside.

2. In the top of a double boiler, or in a heatproof bowl, set over a saucepan of hot, not boiling water, melt chocolate chips, stirring until smooth. Remove from heat and whisk chocolate to cool slightly, about 1 minute. Whisk in butter until melted and blended.

3. Fold whipped cream into the chocolate, one-third at a time, until just blended. Cover and refrigerate for at least 3 hours or until set or for up to 6 hours.

Guacamole (page 107)

Pepper Confetti Salsa (page 108)
and Parsnip Chips (page 171)

Pineapple Mango Salsa (page 118)

Greek Salad Dip (page 53),
Tropical Fruit Salsa (page 127),
and Creamy Watercress Dip (page 26)

Easy Hummus (page 136)

Santorini-Style Fava Spread (page 142)

Black Bean and Salsa Dip (page 145)

Champagne and Raspberry Dip (page 153)

Chips, Crostini, Flatbreads and other Dippers

Salt-Roasted Potatoes

This mouth-watering treatment for new potatoes is a summer staple. Be sure to use good sea salt and don't skimp on the quantity; it's an integral part of the taste sensation. They make a fabulous delivery vehicle for dips such as Springtime Dill Dip (page 25), Creamy Watercress Dip (page 26) or those traditionally served with potatoes such as Mojo de Cilantro (page 20) or Canary Island Red Pepper Mojo (page 10). But they are so tasty, you can also serve them on their own, topped with a dollop of sour cream and a sprinkling of finely snipped chives, if you are so inclined.

Makes 1 serving per potato

Tips

You can precook the potatoes and refrigerate until ready to use. Don't cut them in half until you're ready to finish them.

Don't drown the potatoes in olive oil. You'll need about 1 tbsp (15 mL) per pound (500 g) of potatoes.

• Preheat barbecue grill to high or broiler

1 tbsp	extra virgin olive oil	15 mL
	Fine sea salt	
1 lb	new potatoes, boiled in their skins just until tender (see Tips, left)	500 g

1. In a bowl large enough to accommodate the potatoes, combine olive oil and salt to taste. Cut cooked potatoes in half. Add to bowl and toss to thoroughly coat with mixture.

2. Place potatoes cut side down on grill or broiling pan and cook until beginning to brown, about 5 minutes per side. Let cool slightly. Spear each half with a toothpick and serve.

Roasted Potato Wedges

This falls under the category of "everyone will love." Serve these great roasted wedges with an assortment of dips, from Black Pepper Goat Cheese Dip (page 37) to Nippy Oyster and Bacon Dip (page 80).

Makes 16 wedges

Tip

Play with this recipe to create your own fan favorite. Glaze with maple syrup or drizzle a good-quality white truffle oil over top — or how about some leftover gravy!

- **Preheat oven to 325°F (160°C)**
- **Large ovenproof skillet**

1 lb	russet (Idaho) potatoes (about 2 medium)	500 g
1 tbsp	salt	15 mL
1 tbsp	olive oil	15 mL
1 tbsp	unsalted butter	15 mL
½ tsp	chopped fresh thyme leaves	2 mL
½ tsp	chopped fresh basil leaves	2 mL
½ tsp	freshly ground black pepper	2 mL

1. Using a sharp knife, cut each potato lengthwise into 8 wedges.

2. Place potatoes in a pot and add water to cover. Add salt and bring to a boil over medium heat. Reduce heat and simmer until potatoes are fork tender, about 8 minutes. Drain and pat dry with a towel. Set aside.

3. In skillet, heat oil and butter over medium-high heat. Add potatoes and mix well to coat. Transfer skillet to preheated oven and bake until golden brown and crisp, about 25 minutes. Transfer potatoes to a bowl. Add thyme, basil and pepper. Mix well and serve immediately.

Easy Potato Crisps

These thin slices of roast potatoes make a great base for many spreads. They are particularly good with Smoked Salmon Mousse (page 72) or Dill-Spiked Smoked Trout Spread (page 74).

Makes about 20 crisps

• **Preheat oven to 400°F (200°C)**

| 2 | potatoes, peeled or unpeeled, thinly sliced (⅛ inch/3 mm) | 2 |
| 2 tbsp | extra virgin olive oil | 30 mL |

1. In a bowl, combine potatoes and olive oil. Toss until potatoes are well coated. Place on baking sheet in a single layer and roast in preheated oven, turning once, until potatoes are crisp and browned, about 20 minutes.

Handmade Dippers

While crudités, plain crackers or sliced baguette are almost always appropriate for dipping, from time to time, it can be fun to try something a little different, even if it involves a bit of work. To make your own chips, deep-fry thin slices of plantain (page 167), beets (page 169) or parsnip (page 171) or use Homemade Potato Chips (page 165). Some dips can also double as spreads, so they may make a tasty topping for crêpe-like breads such as Buckwheat Blini (page 178) or Yogurt Flatbread (page 174). Since dips come from so many cultural traditions and contain so many different combinations of ingredients, it can be fun to let your imagination run wild.

Homemade Potato Chips

Vegan Friendly

These chips are extremely versatile. They are particularly delicious with creamy dips such as Caramelized Red Onion Dip (page 40) or Smoky Baked Onion Dip (page 41).

Makes 6 servings

Tip

Cook the chips long enough to ensure they are crisp. They can be browned but still a bit soft in the middle. Turning helps to ensure they cook evenly.

- **Candy/deep-fry thermometer**
- **Food processor**

1½ lbs	potatoes, peeled (about 2 medium)	750 g
2 cups	oil, such as peanut or corn (approx.)	500 mL
	Fine sea salt	

1. In food processor fitted with slicing blade, slice potatoes. Transfer to a large bowl. Cover with cold salted water and soak for 10 minutes. Drain in a colander and rinse thoroughly under cold running water. Place in a salad spinner and dry thoroughly.

2. In a deep skillet, Dutch oven or deep fryer, heat oil over medium-high heat to 350°F (180°C). Add potato slices, in batches, and fry, stirring frequently to keep them separated and turning once to ensure they brown evenly, until golden, about 5 minutes per batch (see Tip, left). Using a slotted spoon, transfer to a paper towel–lined plate. Sprinkle to taste with salt. Repeat with remaining potatoes.

Fresh Corn Cakes

What a glorious showcase for one of the sweetest vegetables around — corn. For a fresh pick-me-up, top with a spoon of sour cream or crème fraîche. To take it to the next level, garnish with a dollop of a savory salsa, such as Roasted Corn Salsa (page 104) or Roasted Red Pepper Salsa (page 98).

Makes about 25 cakes

Tips

If you have problems digesting gluten, substitute an equal quantity of gluten-free all-purpose flour for the regular variety.

Frozen corn is readily available and can be used in place of fresh but should be thoroughly thawed and dried before using.

7 tbsp	all-purpose flour (see Tips, left)	105 mL
1/4 cup	freshly grated Parmesan cheese, preferably Parmigiano-Reggiano	60 mL
1/2 tsp	baking powder	2 mL
1/2 tsp	salt	2 mL
2	eggs	2
1/4 cup	milk	60 mL
2 cups	fresh corn kernels (see Tips, left)	500 mL
2 tbsp	finely chopped red bell pepper	30 mL
1 tbsp	minced garlic	15 mL
1/2 tsp	chopped fresh thyme leaves	2 mL
2	egg whites, at room temperature	2
3 tbsp	unsalted butter, divided	45 mL

1. In a large bowl, combine flour, Parmesan, baking powder and salt. In another bowl, whisk together eggs and milk. Add to flour mixture with corn, bell pepper, garlic and thyme and stir just until blended.

2. In a small bowl, using an electric mixer, beat egg whites until stiff peaks. Fold into batter just until blended. Cover and refrigerate for 1 hour.

3. In a nonstick skillet, melt 1 tbsp (15 mL) of the butter over medium heat. Spoon about $1\frac{1}{2}$ tbsp (22 mL) of batter per cake into the pan. Cook, turning once, until golden brown, 3 to 4 minutes per side. Transfer to a plate. Repeat with remaining batter, adding butter and adjusting heat as necessary between batches. Serve hot.

Green Plantain Chips

These little tidbits are very versatile. They can be eaten on their own, perhaps sprinkled with a cilantro-lime mixture (see Variation, below) and in that case are best served while still warm. They also make a great accompaniment to many salsas, particularly those made with fruit, such as Minty Mango Salsa (page 117) or Tropical Fruit Salsa (page 127), or a cilantro-based salsa, such as Suneeta's Cilantro Mint Chutney (page 109).

Makes about 36 chips

Tip

Green plantains are not easily peeled, unlike their banana relatives. To peel, make a lengthwise slit through the skin with a paring knife, being careful not to cut into the plantain, then lift off the peel.

• **Candy/deep-fry thermometer**

2 cups	oil	500 mL
2	green plantains, peeled and very thinly sliced (see Tip, left)	2
	Salt	

1. In a deep skillet or Dutch oven, heat oil over medium-high heat to 325°F (160°C). (You can also use a deep fryer; follow the manufacturer's instructions.) Fry plantain slices, in batches to avoid crowding, just until they are beginning to turn golden, about $1\frac{1}{2}$ minutes. Using a slotted spoon, remove from oil and transfer to a cutting board. Cover with plastic and pound to about $\frac{1}{4}$-inch (0.5 cm) thickness.

2. Increase heat of oil to 375°F (190°C). Fry pounded slices, in batches, turning if necessary, until golden, 2 to 3 minutes. Transfer to a paper towel–lined platter and sprinkle with salt.

Variation

Cilantro-Topped Tostanes: Do not sprinkle chips with salt. In a small bowl, combine $\frac{1}{4}$ cup (60 mL) finely chopped cilantro leaves, 1 tbsp (15 mL) freshly squeezed lime juice and 1 tsp (5 mL) salt. If you like a bit of heat, add minced jalapeño pepper, to taste. Stir well. Sprinkle over warm chips and serve immediately.

Spicy Kale Chips

Finally a chip with little guilt! Kale chips are so easy to make and can be made with so many different flavorings — be creative. They're a lot like Homemade Potato Chips (page 165) — you can't just stop at one, so be sure to make a lot.

Makes about 10 servings

Tips

Lacinto kale (also known as black or dinosaur kale) is good for making chips because its long, relatively solid leaves allow for the creation of a "chip" that has enough heft to be used as a dipper.

If you are a vegan, use unbleached organic sugar to ensure it has not been filtered through bone char.

- **Preheat oven to 300°F (150°C)**
- **Baking sheet, lined with parchment paper**

1	bunch kale (about 8 oz/250 g)	1
2 tbsp	olive oil	30 mL
½ tsp	salt	2 mL
¼ tsp	chipotle powder	1 mL
¼ tsp	granulated sugar (see Tips, left)	1 mL

1. Remove tough stems from kale and discard. Tear leaves into bite-size pieces (you should have about 2 cups/ 500 mL). In a bowl, combine oil, salt, chipotle powder and sugar. Toss kale pieces in mixture to coat. Spread kale on prepared baking sheet, ensuring the pieces aren't overlapping as this will prevent the chips from crisping (use more baking sheets or bake in batches if necessary). Bake in preheated oven until crisp, about 15 minutes. Let cool to room temperature before serving.

Beet Chips

Vegan Friendly

Be sure to wear gloves for this recipe or your hands will be purple for your dinner party. These are a great base for many dips and salsas. For visual appeal, top a chip with Roasted Corn Salsa (page 104) or Roasted Beet Salsa (page 94). The yellow corn contrasts beautifully with the purple chip.

Makes 25 to 30 chips

Tips

If you're using a deep fryer, follow the manufacturer's instructions.

Although frying tastes great, a healthier option is to bake these chips. Preheat oven to 375°F (190°C). Toss sliced beets with 1 tbsp (15 mL) olive oil and spread chips out on a parchment paper–lined baking sheet. Bake in a preheated oven until golden brown and crisp, turning every 15 minutes, about 50 minutes. Transfer to a bowl. Combine with almond mixture and toss lightly to coat. Let cool until crisp.

Chips keep in an airtight container for up to 1 day.

- **Candy/deep-fry thermometer**

	Oil	
1 tsp	finely ground toasted almonds	5 mL
¼ tsp	salt	1 mL
⅛ tsp	ground cinnamon	0.5 mL
1	large beet, peeled	1

1. Fill a deep fryer, deep heavy pot or deep skillet with 3 inches (7.5 cm) of oil and heat over medium-high heat to 375°F (190°C) (see Tips, left).

2. In a large bowl, combine almonds, salt and cinnamon and mix well to combine. Set aside.

3. Using a mandoline, a food processor fitted with a slicer blade or a very sharp knife, thinly slice beet into 25 to 30 slices. (They should resemble the thickness of potato chips.) Using tongs, gently place 6 chips at a time into the hot oil and deep-fry, turning once, until golden brown and crispy, 2 to 3 minutes. Using a slotted spoon, remove from oil and add to almond mixture, tossing to coat lightly. Let cool on paper towel to absorb excess oil. As chips cool they will become crispy. Serve immediately.

Taro Root Chips

Although not widely used in North America, this potato-like tuber is very familiar to many cultures all over the world. Taro chips become crisper than any potato chip could ever claim to be. Give them a try. They are wonderful with Tropical Fruit Salsa (page 127) or any fruit salsa for that matter.

Makes about 25 to 30

Tips

If you're using a deep fryer, follow the manufacturer's instructions.

Although frying tastes great, a healthier option is to bake these chips. Preheat oven to 375°F (190°C). Toss sliced taro with 1 tbsp (15 mL) olive oil and spread chips out on a parchment paper–lined baking sheet. Bake in a preheated oven until golden brown and crisp, turning every 15 minutes, for about 50 minutes. Transfer to a bowl. Combine with dill mixture and toss lightly to coat. Let cool until crisp.

Chips keep in an airtight container for up to 1 day.

- **Candy/deep-fry thermometer**

	Peanut oil	
¼ tsp	salt	1 mL
⅛ tsp	ground dill seed	0.5 mL
1	large taro root, peeled	1

1. Fill a deep fryer, deep heavy pot or deep skillet with 3 inches (7.5 cm) of oil and heat to 375°F (190°C) (see Tips, left).

2. In a large bowl, combine salt and dill seed. Mix well and set aside.

3. Using a mandoline, a food processor fitted with the slicer blade or a very sharp knife, thinly slice taro into 25 to 30 slices. (They should resemble the thickness of potato chips.) Using tongs, gently place 6 chips at a time into the hot oil and deep-fry, turning once, until golden brown and crispy, 2 to 3 minutes. Using a slotted spoon, remove from oil and add to dill mixture, tossing to coat lightly. Let cool on paper towel to absorb excess oil. As chips cool they will become crispy. Serve immediately.

Parsnip Chips

Parsnips create spectacular sweet and savory crisps. They are particularly delicious with dips or salsas containing mushrooms and/or tomatoes, such as Mushroom Tomato Spread (page 23) or Roasted Tomato Dip (page 22).

Makes about 25 to 30

Tips

If you're using a deep fryer, follow the manufacturer's instructions.

Although frying tastes great, a healthier option is to bake these chips. Preheat oven to 375°F (190°C). Toss sliced parsnips with 1 tbsp (15 mL) olive oil and spread chips out on a parchment paper–lined baking sheet. Bake in a preheated oven until golden brown and crisp, turning every 15 minutes, for about 50 minutes. Transfer to a bowl, add salt and toss lightly to coat. Let cool until crisp.

Chips keep in an airtight container for up to 1 day.

- **Candy/deep-fry thermometer**

	Peanut oil	
2	large parsnips, peeled	2
¼ tsp	salt	1 mL

1. Fill a deep fryer, deep heavy pot or deep skillet with 3 inches (7.5 cm) of oil and heat to 375°F (190°C) (see Tips, left)

2. Using a mandoline, a food processor fitted with the slicer blade or a very sharp knife, thinly slice parsnips into 25 to 30 slices. (They should resemble the thickness of potato chips.) Using tongs, gently place 6 chips at a time into the hot oil and deep-fry, turning once, until golden brown and crispy, 2 to 3 minutes. Using a slotted spoon, remove from oil. Transfer to a bowl, add salt and toss lightly to coat. Let cool on paper towel to absorb excess oil. As chips cool they will become crispy. Serve immediately.

Variation

Sweet Parsnip Chips: Here is a way to turn parsnip chips into a healthy dessert offering. Substitute 1 tbsp (15 mL) confectioner's (icing) sugar for the salt. Or melt 2 oz (60 g) semisweet chocolate and dip cooled parsnip chips about one-quarter of the way into chocolate. Let cool on a parchment paper–lined baking sheet until chocolate is set.

Crisp Pita Bread

Crisp pita bread, seasoned or unseasoned, makes a nice accompaniment for many spreads and dips. Serve it plain, or choose seasonings that complement what you are serving. Greek-style pita, which doesn't have a pocket, produces a nicely crisp bread. If you're looking for a "chip"–type dipper, use pita with a pocket and separate the tops from bottoms before baking.

Makes 32 crisps

Tip

Most pita bread contains gluten. However, more and more gluten-free versions are becoming available, so if you have trouble digesting gluten, it's worth searching out a gluten-free alternative to prepare this recipe and any of the variations.

• **Preheat oven to 400°F (200°C)**

8	Greek-style pita breads (no pockets)	8
	Extra virgin olive oil	

1. Brush pita on both sides with olive oil. Place on baking sheets top side down and bake in preheated oven for 5 minutes.

2. Flip over and bake until pita is crisping and turning golden, for 5 minutes more. Let cool slightly and cut each pita into quarters.

Variations

Grilled Pita Bread: If you prefer a slightly smoky flavor, follow above instructions but grill pita on a hot barbecue, adjusting timing if necessary.

Mediterranean-Spiced Crisp Pita Bread: Follow instructions for Crisp or Grilled Pita Bread, completing Step 1. Remove sheets from oven. After turning pitas, sprinkle each with about ½ tsp (2 mL) dried Italian seasoning. Complete Step 2.

Middle Eastern–Spiced Crisp Pita Bread: In a small dry skillet, combine 1 tbsp (15 mL) cumin seeds and 1 tsp (5 mL) coriander seeds. Place over medium heat and toast, stirring, until fragrant, about 3 minutes. Transfer to a mortar or spice grinder and grind. Set aside. Follow instructions for Crisp or Grilled Pita Bread, completing Step 1. Remove sheets from oven. After turning pitas, sprinkle each with about ½ tsp (2 mL) of the spice mix. Complete Step 2.

Crisp Pita Bread with Dukkah: Follow instructions for Crisp or Grilled Pita Bread, completing Step 1. Remove sheets from oven. After turning pitas, sprinkle each with about ½ tsp (2 mL) Dukkah. Complete Step 2. Dukkah, a Middle Eastern condiment, is available in specialty markets.

Pita Chips: Substitute 4 pita with pockets for Greek-style pita bread. Separate layers of pitas horizontally before beginning the recipe. Proceed as for Crisp or Grilled Pita Bread, adding any of the seasonings above, if desired.

Breads for Dipping

Simply prepared bread, such as sliced baguette or warm pita bread, or crackers, are among the most popular accompaniments for dips and salsas because they are easy-to-serve and versatile, blending as they do with a wide variety of textures and flavors. Breadsticks, crostini, either store-bought or homemade (page 176), and chunks of focaccia (particularly tasty with Warm Anchovy Dip, page 72) are also good choices. If you're looking for something a bit more elaborate, try seasoning pita bread (see Variations, left) or make Pita Chips (see Variation, above), Bagel Chips (page 177) or your own flatbread such as Yogurt Flatbread (page 174). More and more bakeries are providing gluten-free versions of traditional breads, so if you have trouble digesting gluten, it's worth seeking out a gluten-free alternative. Tortilla chips (which are made from tortillas, Mexican flatbread, should be gluten-free) are probably the most popular dippers for any type of salsa.

Yogurt Flatbread

Warm from the oven, these little flatbreads are yummy on their own, but if you're so inclined, use them as a dipper (try Yogurt Mint Chutney, page 110) or top with a dollop of chutney (Suneeta's Cilantro Mint Chutney, page 109 or Date and Tamarind Chutney, page 158). They also make a good base for spreads such as Smoked Salmon Mousse (page 72) or Dill-Spiked Smoked Trout Spread (page 74).

Makes about 2½ dozen

Tips

Be sure to use good sea salt, such as fleur de sel to finish your bread. Refined table salt has a bitter acrid taste.

You can purchase za'atar in specialty spice shops or make your own. *To make za'atar:* In a small bowl, combine 2 tbsp (30 mL) fresh thyme leaves, 1 tbsp (15 mL) toasted sesame seeds and 1 tsp (5 mL) each ground sumac and coarse sea salt.

To toast sesame seeds: Place seeds in a dry skillet over medium heat and cook, stirring, just until they begin to brown. Immediately transfer to a bowl; once they start to brown they burn quickly.

- **Preheat oven to 350°F (180°C)**
- **2½-inch (6 cm) round cutter**
- **Baking sheets, lined with parchment paper**

2 cups	all-purpose flour	500 mL
1 tsp	baking powder	5 mL
½ tsp	salt	2 mL
1 cup	plain yogurt	250 mL
2 tbsp	extra virgin olive oil	30 mL
	Course sea salt	

1. In a bowl, combine flour, baking powder and salt. Add yogurt and, using a wooden spoon, mix as well as you can. Then use your hands to knead until a soft dough forms. Cover and let rest at room temperature for 1 hour.

2. Divide dough into quarters. Working with one piece at a time, on a lightly floured board, roll out dough to a ⅛-inch (3 mm) thickness. Using cutter, cut into rounds and place on prepared sheets. Repeat until all the dough has been cut into circles, re-rolling scraps.

3. Bake in preheated oven until nicely puffed, about 15 minutes. Remove from oven and preheat broiler. Place flatbreads under broiler until lightly browned. Brush with olive oil and sprinkle with salt. Serve warm.

Variations

Gluten-Free Yogurt Flatbread: Substitute ¾ cup (175 mL) each sorghum and fine brown rice flour, ½ cup (125 mL) tapioca flour, 1 tsp (5 mL) each xanthan gum and gluten-free baking powder, for the all-purpose flour and regular baking powder.

Za'atar-Spiked Flatbread: After the flatbreads have been brushed with olive oil, sprinkle with za'atar (see Tips, left). Then finish with salt to taste.

Herb-Spiked Flatbread: In a small bowl, combine 1 tbsp (15 mL) minced fresh thyme leaves and 1 tsp (5 mL) finely grated lemon zest. After the flatbreads have been brushed with olive oil, sprinkle with the mixture, then finish with salt to taste.

Crudités for Dipping

Crudités are cut-up vegetables used for dipping. Today, the selection of vegetables in the market — more and more of which are washed and precut — makes it convenient to use these healthful ingredients as crudités. Popular choices are broccoli and cauliflower florets, peeled baby carrots, spears of Belgian endive and cherry tomatoes. If you're looking for something a little different, try thin slices of fennel, small radicchio leaves or hearts of romaine, blanched asparagus, radishes, including thin slices of peeled daikon, or even sliced canned hearts of palm. And don't forget old standbys such as carrot or celery sticks and thinly sliced cucumber or zucchini. Another favorite is blanched Brussels sprouts, which are particularly good with strongly flavored dips, such as Warm Anchovy Dip (page 72). Although they don't actually qualify as crudités, when new potatoes are abundant in farmers' markets, we love to cook them in boiling salted water until tender, spear them on wooden skewers, and dunk in unctuous concoctions such as Caramelized Onion Dip (page 39) or Bubbling Bacon and Horseradish Dip (page 82).

Basic Crostini

Crostini means different things to different people. In French cooking, they are often fried cubes of seasoned bread that are used as a garnish. Here, we are defining Basic Crostini as sliced baguette that is brushed with olive oil, perhaps seasoned with garlic, toasted, and used as a base for canapés. Basic Crostini can use used as a base for a wide variety of dips and spreads such as Roasted Beet and Goat Cheese Spread (page 56), Black Pepper Goat Cheese Dip (page 37) and Pimento Cheese (page 61).

Makes 8 crostini

Tip

This basic recipe for crostini can be doubled, tripled or quadrupled to suit your entertaining needs. Crostini can be made ahead. After cooling, store in an airtight container for up to 3 days.

- **Preheat broiler**

| 8 | slices baguette (each ¼ inch/0.5 cm thick) Olive oil (see Tips, below) | 8 |

1. Brush baguette slices lightly with olive oil on both sides. Place under preheated broiler and toast until golden, turning once, about 2 minutes per side.

Variation

Gluten-Free Crostini: Substitute gluten-free baguette for the regular version.

Seasoning Crostini

Seasoning crostini lightly with garlic is common. If you prefer a hint of garlic on your crostini, an easy way to achieve this is to brush them with garlic-infused olive oil. *To make garlic-infused olive oil:* Combine ¼ cup (60 mL) olive oil and 1 tbsp (15 mL) puréed or finely minced garlic (see below). Cover and let steep at room temperature for several hours. Strain through a fine sieve or funnel lined with a paper coffee filter. Discard garlic. Be sure to use the oil immediately as infused oils are a favored medium for bacteria growth.

Puréed garlic is preferable to minced garlic when making an infused oil because it integrates more fully into the oil. To purée garlic, use a fine, sharp-toothed grater, such as those made by Microplane.

Bagel Chips

This crisp versatile chip is delicious all on its own and even better topped with a tasty dip or spread, such as Kentucky Beer Cheese (page 62) or Homemade Herb Cheese (page 59).

(page 62)

Makes about 16 chips

Tip

Your bakery will often have a slicer and would be more than happy to slice your day-old bagels, however a good serrated knife would do the trick.

- **Preheat oven to 350°F (180°C)**
- **Baking sheet, lined with parchment paper**

2	bagels (your favorite variety)	2
1	clove garlic, cut in half	1
2 tbsp	olive oil	30 mL
½ tsp	salt	2 mL

1. Thinly slice each bagel into 8 thin slices. Place on prepared baking sheet. Rub garlic on both sides of bagel slices.

2. In a bowl, combine oil and salt, mixing to dissolve salt. Liberally brush both sides of bagel slices with mixture. Place on prepared baking sheet and bake in preheated oven until golden brown and crisp, about 12 minutes. Serve immediately or store in an airtight container for up to 1 week.

Variation

Gluten-Free Bagel Chips: Substitute gluten-free bagels for the regular version.

Buckwheat Blini

Blini have luxurious overtones because they are traditionally served with the best caviar. While you can certainly top these with a dollop of beluga (if you're lucky enough to have some), they are also delicious with Smoked Salmon Mousse (page 72) or Dill-Spiked Smoked Trout Spread (page 74). You can also top them with thin slices of smoked salmon, a squirt of fresh lemon juice, a spoonful of crème fraîche, liberal amounts of freshly ground black pepper and a sprinkling of finely snipped chives.

Makes about 36 blini

Tips

Blini are best served immediately after cooking, but you can make them up to 1 day ahead. Cover and refrigerate cooked blini. Brush with extra virgin olive oil or melted butter and heat in 325°F (160°C) oven for about 10 minutes.

If you are a vegetarian, use unbleached organic sugar to ensure it has not been filtered through bone char.

- **Preheat oven to 200°F (100°C)**

2 tsp	granulated sugar (see Tips, left)	10 mL
1 cup	warm whole milk (about 100°F/38°C)	250 mL
1 tsp	active dry yeast	5 mL
½ cup	all-purpose flour	125 mL
½ cup	buckwheat flour	125 mL
½ tsp	salt	2 mL
1	egg, beaten	1
2 tbsp	melted unsalted butter	30 mL
	Oil	

1. In a bowl, combine sugar and warm milk. Stir to dissolve sugar. Sprinkle yeast evenly over top and set aside until frothy, about 10 minutes.

2. In another bowl, combine all-purpose and buckwheat flours and salt. Stir well. Add yeast mixture and mix well. Add egg and butter and mix well. Cover with plastic wrap and set aside in a warm, draft-free place until mixture rises slightly and top is quite bubbly, about 1 hour.

3. Brush nonstick skillet lightly with oil and place over medium heat. Spoon 1 tbsp (15 mL) of batter per blin and cook until bubbles form on the top and underside is brown, about 30 seconds. Flip and cook until golden on the bottom, about 30 seconds. Transfer to a baking sheet as completed and keep warm in preheated oven. Grease skillet and adjust heat between batches, as necessary. Serve warm, with your favorite topping.

Variation

Gluten-Free Buckwheat Blini: Substitute ½ cup (125 mL) sorghum flour plus 1 tbsp (15 mL) cornstarch for the all-purpose flour.

Cheese Arepas

Arepas are a South American (mainly Colombian or Venezuelan) fast food. Making them the traditional way, from scratch with white corn grits can be tricky, but if you have access to arepa flour, which is a form of precooked cornmeal, they are a snap. They are great if you're looking for something that's tasty and a bit different and are particularly delicious topped with a dollop of a complementary salsa such as Fresh Tomato Salsa (page 86), Avocado Corn Salsa (page 106), Avocado Black Bean Salsa (page 146) or Fresh Salsa Verde (page 89).

Makes about 18

Tip

Arepa flour, which is made from corn, is available in well-stocked supermarkets or stores specializing in Latin American products.

1 cup	arepa flour (see Tip, left)	250 mL
1 cup	shredded mozzarella or Monterey Jack cheese	250 mL
½ tsp	salt	2 mL
½ to 1	jalapeño pepper, seeded and minced (see Tips, page 180)	½ to 1
1 cup	warm milk	250 mL
1	egg yolk, beaten	1
¼ cup	oil, divided (approx.)	60 mL

1. In a bowl, combine arepa flour, cheese, salt and jalapeño to taste. Stir well. Add milk and egg yolk and mix until incorporated. Using your hands, knead lightly to form a soft dough.

2. Working with about 2 tbsp (30 mL) of dough at a time, shape into a ball, then flatten into a round, about 2 inches (5 cm) in diameter. Repeat until all dough is used up. You should have about 18 rounds.

3. In a large skillet, heat 2 tbsp (30 mL) of the oil over medium heat. Add arepas, in batches, being careful not to overcrowd the pan, and cook until nicely browned on one side, about 2 minutes. Flip, press down with the back of a spatula and cook until browned on other side, about 2 minutes. Transfer to a serving plate and keep warm. Repeat until all arepas are cooked, adding more oil as necessary between batches. Serve warm.

Corn Arepas

Make these tasty treats when fresh corn is in season. They are delicious on their own and superb topped with a fresh salsa, such as Shrimp Salsa (page 111), Avocado Corn Salsa (page 106), Avocado Black Bean Salsa (page 146), Fresh Tomato Salsa (page 86) or Fresh Salsa Verde (page 89).

Makes about 18

Tips

Arepa flour, which is made from corn, is available in well-stocked supermarkets or stores specializing in Latin American products.

Use a whole jalapeño for a spicier arepa. If you are true heat seeker, leave the veins and seeds in before chopping the pepper.

1 tbsp	unsalted butter	15 mL
1	shallot, finely chopped	1
½ to 1	jalapeño pepper, seeded and minced, optional (see Tips, left)	½ to 1
1 cup	corn kernels, thawed if frozen (1 cob)	250 mL
2 tbsp	heavy or whipping (35%) cream	30 mL
1 tbsp	finely chopped fresh oregano leaves	15 mL
½ tsp	salt, or to taste	2 mL
	Freshly ground black pepper	
1 cup	arepa flour (see Tips, left)	250 mL
1 cup	water	250 mL
¼ cup	oil, divided	60 mL

1. In a small skillet, melt butter over medium heat. Add shallot and jalapeño to taste, if using, and cook, stirring, until shallot is softened, about 3 minutes. Stir in corn and cream. Bring to boil, reduce heat to low, cover and simmer until corn is tender, about 4 minutes. Add oregano, salt, and pepper to taste, and stir well. Transfer to a bowl.

2. Stir in arepa flour. Add water and mix until incorporated. Using your hands, knead to form a soft dough.

3. Working with about 2 tbsp (30 mL) of dough at a time, shape into a ball, then flatten into a round about 2 inches (5 cm) in diameter. Repeat until all dough is used up. You should have about 18 rounds.

4. In a large skillet, heat 2 tbsp (30 mL) of the oil over medium heat. Add arepas, in batches, being careful not to overcrowd the pan, and cook until nicely browned on one side, about 2 minutes. Flip, press down with the back of a spatula and cook until browned on the other side, about 2 minutes. Transfer to a serving plate and keep warm. Repeat until all arepas are cooked, adding more oil as necessary between batches. Serve warm.

Acknowledgments

As always, thanks to my husband and greatest fan, Bob Dees. Life wouldn't be nearly as much fun without you. Also to Marian Jarkovich, Nina McCreath and Martine Quibell for their professional commitment, which is always above and beyond the call of duty. Also to Audrey King, my longtime recipe tester, whose exactitude is consistently exemplary. To the team at PageWave Graphics — Kevin Cockburn, Joseph Gisini and Daniella Zanchetta, food stylist Kathryn Robertson, prop stylist Charlene Erricson and photographer Colin Erricson, for making my recipes look so delicious and my books look so beautiful. And last, but certainly not least, to my editor Carol Sherman, who always manages to maintain her poise and terrific sense of humor, even in the middle of impending catastrophe.

— Judith Finlayson

Without question this book has been a labor of love. I have a newfound respect for authors. A huge thank you to Bob Dees for this exceptional opportunity. To Judith Finlayson and Carol Sherman, thank you for your patience and direction throughout this process. To my friends who are fighting, keep up the good fight, you're stronger than I could ever be. To those friends who have lost their fight you will be in our hearts always.

To Tamar, Jonah and Jamie, thank you for putting up with the good, bad and ugly (read cranky) me. I love you very much. You are my life.

— Chef Jordan Wagman

Index

Library and Archives Canada Cataloguing in Publication

Finlayson, Judith, author
    150 best dips & salsas : plus recipes for chips, flatbreads and more / Judith Finlayson & Jordan Wagman.

Includes index.
ISBN 978-0-7788-0485-7 (pbk.)

1. Dips (Appetizers). 2. Salsas (Cooking). 3. Cookbooks.
I. Wagman, Jordan, author II. Title. III. Title: One hundred and fifty best dips & salsas.
IV. Title: 150 best dips and salsas. V. Title: One hundred and fifty best dips and salsas.

TX740.F5294 2014   641.8'12   C2014-903337-0